THE CHILD INSIDE

ISBN-10: 0615503527
EAN-13: 9780615503523

THE CHILD INSIDE

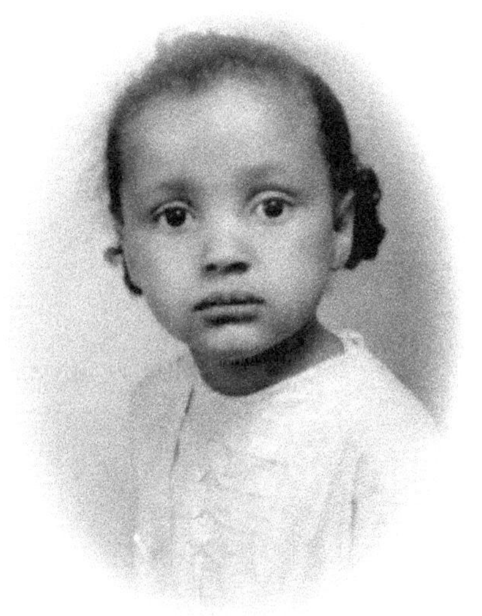

NANCY CAROL VEGA

THE CHILD INSIDE

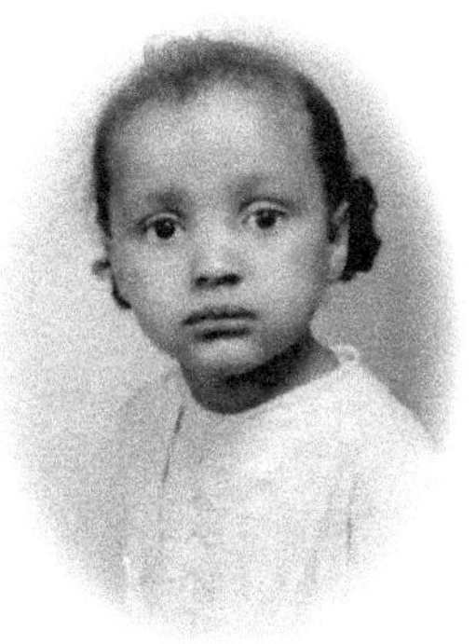

A true, shocking, action-packed, thrilling story of thirteen children's struggle for survival in a sadistically controlled environment.

WARNING: Portions of this book may be unsuitable for children. Parental discretion advised.

by Nancy Carol Vega

Contents

Chapter One	Early Childhood Abuse	Page 1
Chapter Two	Dad's Tight Fisted Control	Page 5
Chapter Three	The Name of the Game Is Survival	Page 11
Chapter Four	Holiday Celebrations	Page 17
Chapter Five	Marketing (the Ups and Downs)	Page 23
Chapter Six	Incest and Its Effect	Page 27
Chapter Seven	Drugs and Busts, Smoking and Boozing It Up	Page 37
Chapter Eight	Making It on My Own	Page 45
Chapter Nine	The Wedding, Reception, and Married Life at Dad's	Page 61
Chapter Ten	Frank and I on Our Own Again	Page 73
Chapter Eleven	Satan's Antics	Page 85
Chapter Twelve	The Funeral March	Page 93

THIS IS A TRUE STORY

I DEDICATE THIS BOOK TO ALL

THE ABUSED CHILDREN

OF THE WORLD.

Introduction

Looking back to that day in 1976, when Nancy first entered my life, a smile comes over my face. My six-year-old son was playing in the back yard. Unfortunately, (or so it seemed at the time) he got carried away throwing rocks over our back fence into the alley. In the process he hit Nancy's four-year-old daughter in the head, causing her mother to become outraged and approach me in hysterics. I firmly but softly reprimanded my son, and I apologized to the mother. Yes, the mother was Nancy. Little did I know this was to be a lifelong friendship. It wasn't until recent years that Nancy shared with me her recollections of that first encounter. She said she was ready to pull my hair out!

Over the fourteen years of our friendship I have seen the Lord Jesus gently woo Nancy into His kingdom. After a long series of events, and a couple different cult religions, Nancy came to Jesus in 1984. Over the years of our friendship, Nancy shared with me pieces of the story of her family and childhood. When she approached me in January, 1989, and I volunteered to assist her in writing this autobiography, I was completely ignorant as to what was about to be revealed to me. Even though at the time she came to me in shame and embarrassment, the secrets locked in her heart were humiliating to disclose even to a trusted friend.

Praise God for His healing power of love that flowed between us! The anointing of God was present to break the yoke. I feel honored to have been available to experience this miracle. As the months progressed, I saw Nancy transformed from glory to glory. God used our collaboration on this book as a therapeutic process to produce inner healing in Nancy.

As the reader enters the pages of this book, please keep in mind that this account is intended to reveal the works of Satan in the belief that people both young and old may be delivered from bondage. In Matthew 11:28 and 29, it says: "Come unto Me all you who labor and are heavy laden, and I will give you rest. Take My yoke upon you and learn from Me, for I am gentle and lowly in heart, and you will find rest for your souls. For My yoke is easy and My burden is light." My prayer is that many may be set free and come into the saving knowledge of our Lord Jesus Christ by reading Nancy's life story. God bless you.

Joan.

Preface

About five years ago I received the Lord Jesus Christ as my personal Savior. My Lord delivered me from a background which was ugly and distasteful. Praise God I was set free from bondage—or at least I thought so.

As time passed, the fruit of the Holy Spirit began to produce in my life. God was transforming me into a new creature in Christ Jesus. (Phil 1:6 "Being confident of this very thing, that He who has begun a good work in you will complete it until the day of Jesus Christ.") Such a change took place in me that I thought my ugly past had vanished from my memory. Little did I realize that twenty-five years of the past was cemented in my heart. The cleansing was just beginning.

There were times when strange feelings came over me, causing me to run to my bedroom and asking everyone to leave me alone. When asked what was the problem, I could not explain, nor did I understand it myself. Something from the dark spirit realm was haunting me. These spells could last for hours, or sometimes even months. A few times I locked myself inside the house for up to a year with the curtains drawn. Our three elementary-age schoolchildren did the grocery shopping at the supermarket. When I finally did take the children clothes shopping, I remember being shocked at the high prices of clothing.

One day I was motivated by the Spirit to write about my life experiences. While attempting to write, I saw in a vision my heart broken but with a thick layer of cement around it. Inside the crack were people pointing a finger at me. Something that could have felt like maggots began gnawing at the flesh of my heart as I cried out to God in agony to for His healing power to touch me and burn off the maggots. Praise God, He did!

A few days later, again while working on this book, terror struck me; my recollections were unbearable. It felt as though six large knives had been stuck into my heart and I fell onto my bed immobilized with extreme pain, thinking that I was going to die. The intensity subsided within a half hour, but the pain still remained in my heart for another two weeks, feeling as though my heart was raw flesh stripped of any covering. At one point I wanted to see a doctor to find out if I really had a physical heart problem, but did not. The pain began to go away, but the struggling with my unfolding past had only just begun.

One morning about four o'clock I awoke thinking that the Lord was calling me to my morning prayer time. I felt the presence of a huge black monster in the form of a shadow that seemed to say to me, "I have given you rotten, moldy, and wormy candy to eat—how dare you try and vomit it up!" I got out of bed, and walked through the dark room into the dinning room, crying out to God, "Create in me a clean heart." I then addressed the devil: "On the cross He sealed my pardon!"

I walked into our bedroom one evening I saw a vision of my father's head rolling off the bed; I remembered the unreasonable outrages, I threw things at the windows, violently attempting to stab my husband with a knife, the screams, the crying spells that last sometimes for hours; and dealing with our three high school-age children who, when they brought their friends home, said "Hey, dude, what's with your mom?" Our children would say to their friends, "Our mom is writing a book, and she is just tripping."

Evil spirits latched onto my body, causing me to act and speak crazy things to my family; the hardest part was admitting that I had allowed such entities to get that near to me. Upon admitting this phenomenon and rebuking it in the name of our Lord Jesus Christ, I would pass out for hours.

My husband and my best friend, Joan, asked me why I was taking it so badly—it happened twenty five years ago?" I responded, "No, it just happened to me. These hidden secrets were locked up inside of me all these years, and are finally being released."

As the healing process continued in my heart, the glory of the Lord magnified; sensing His presence and ministering angels surrounded me in a very real way. Taking a break from writing this book, I rested on the bed and called upon the Lord. The room became very bright, and appeared to be lifting up from its foundation,and I fell into a deep sleep. I awoke experiencing a beautiful clean feeling all over my body. For the first time in my life I was cleansed!

The following Sunday when I went to church, one of the many pastors looked at me and ran off the stage in fright. The senior pastor looked at me several times in amazement, knowing that I had been with God, and that the glory of the Lord was upon me. They and other church members knew that I had passed through the fire and was purified. Praise God forevermore!

Special Thanks

First of all, I want to thank the Lord for showing me that I needed deliverance and for carrying me through this ordeal. The very real sense of Your Presence throughout these past few months has given me joy unspeakable.

I want to thank my husband for the encouragement and support that he gave me during the crucial time of writing this book. Thank you, Frank, for the boxes of candy, the food that was catered in, the countless breakfasts in Malibu at six o'clock in the morning, and the constant reassurance that nothing from my past could change your love for me. I thank you for your gentleness during my outrages, for consoling our children when I was irrational, for substituting in my Sunday school class when I needed to stay home, and for openly sharing in my past hurts.

I thank you, Joan, for the love, kindness, understanding, and friendship you showed me during this time and for assisting me with this project, even though our many years of friendship ended the day this book was completed. Your words to me were, "Either this story is true, or you have one hell of an imagination."

I still love you.

The Picture On The Cover Of This Book

Mother had only a few pictures of us children that Dad allowed her to keep. Among these pictures, there were none of me as a baby or a young child. When I asked her why she had no pictures of me, she replied that Dad sent all the pictures of me away. I was disturbed about that, and desperately wanted to know what I had looked like.

I was in the eleventh grade when my first child was born. My babysitter moved away, and out of desperation, I went to Grandma's home, the only relative in town, and asked her if she would babysit for me, so that I could attend school. Through some act of God, she agreed, until I could find another babysitter. Thrilled that she was needed, she enjoyed babysitting him for two months; and she was sad when I found a new babysitter.

One day after school I went to pick up my baby and found Grandma busy in her bedroom. I entered the room and to my surprise I discovered a picture of me sitting on her dresser. Not believing my eyes, I began to reach for the picture, as she said with a very harsh voice, "Don't you be looking at that picture, and don't you be touching it, neither. Don't you be touching anything in this room!" I never forgot that picture, something I wanted to have so badly; remembering the day that picture was taken, pleading to Mom to please make my hair look pretty, because today I am going to have my picture taken. She did not grant my request; unlike my sisters, my hair was not long and beautiful and down to my waist, so she took no interest in grooming me, and that is why I look so sad in the picture.

About seven years later, during Grandma's vacation to California to visit the family, I asked her to duplicate the picture of me that I had seen in her bedroom and told her I would pay her for the expense. She said that there was no price on the picture, and that she could not do that favor for me.

After that, I felt only bitterness towards her, stating that she no longer existed and that my children would never know or learn of her. I kept my promise.

Four years later Grandma was in town, and my three children walked past her without knowing who she was—and she didn't know them.

A few months later I received a phone call from her. "Now what is all this business about, you not speaking to me all these years? What is all that about?" I answered, "The picture. Remember the picture I asked you to duplicate for me, and you said 'No'?" She said, "Oh, that! Why didn't you say so? I'll mail it to you today." She did!

Four months later she passed away.

1. Susan	Mentally disturbed, tormented by demons, suicidal.
2. Vicki	Evil.
3. Jonathan	Slim, handsome, quiet, soft-spoken, talented.
4. James	Mean-spirited, brutal fool.
5. Kelly	Living in an imaginary world.
6. Peter	Illiterate.
7. Nancy	Defiant
8. Sally	Corrupt.
9. Joseph	Worked hard at a young age.
10. Dorothy	Disoriented.
11. Latasha	Mentally slow.
12. Cindy	Young victim
13. Tonya	Young victim

CHAPTER ONE

Early Childhood Abuse

One of my first recollections of Dad's discipline stands out vividly in my mind. In 1958, I was six years old and living in the Dayton Street Projects in Newark, New Jersey, when a neighborhood woman informed my father that she overheard me use a curse word while I was playing outside. Once I was inside our apartment, Dad approached me in a rage and punched me in the mouth, causing my front teeth to become loose and to bleed. He proceeded to beat my body unmercifully. To illustrate this scene better, keep in mind that he was a very large man, about six feet two inches tall, and I was a skinny little girl. I stood there in shock as Mom approached me with soothing arms, gently wiping the blood from my mouth. A few minutes passed, then Dad called me to him. I assumed he was calling me out of compassion, but little did I know. When I reached his side, he shoved a large bar of soap into my little mouth, and my loose teeth stuck to the bar. This was typical of Dad's discipline.

Soon after this incident, Dad was forced to flee from Jersey to New York because he was sought by the police for child molestation and child abuse. Susan and her boyfriend Jose, now her husband, reported him to the police. Dad escorted Susan to the drive-in movies while Mom stayed home to care for the other ten children. When he found out that she had a boyfriend, he took her front false teeth away, which triggered the police report. He also punched her front teeth out because she had invited a boy home from school to do homework together. Each of them sat at the head of the table. Upon seeing that, when the boy left, Dad punched Susan in the mouth, causing her to lose her front teeth. Little did he know, the boy was a homosexual. Susan kept him as a lifetime friend.

Needless to say, Dad was in trouble and abandoned the family. Mother would sneak visits to see him as often as she could, leaving us in Susan's and her boyfriend's care. Susan locked all of us in a room, for the duration of Mom's absence. This way she could be alone with her boyfriend and the apartment would stay clean.

After a year of Mom's New York trips, she moved the family to Bay Shore, Long Island. Grandpa, whom I had little memory of, had passed away, and Grandma probably gave Mother money for a down payment on a house; and possibly Dad's rich witchcraft specialist sister, whom he stayed with as a fugitive, helped him out with some money. Either way, it was certain that Mom's income from scrubbing floors could not have made the move possible.

However, not all of us moved to Bay Shore. Susan got married at sixteen, Vicky did the same when she was fifteen, and I, seven years old, was left with the recently widowed Grandma, a mean, hateful, self-centered woman, playing the role of a good Baptist Christian on Sunday morning who during the week was the harlot for the neighborhood men who frequented the tavern next door.

One evening when I was left alone, I went in search of Grandma and found her at the tavern next door, sitting on the lap of an African American man. I fled before she could discover that I had witnessed the reason for my many lonely nights.

One night when Grandma was at the tavern, a friend of hers—a large fat black man—paid me a visit. I told him that Grandma was not here, which he probably already knew. He entered the house and put me on his lap and touched my vagina. I was uncomfortable about telling Grandma about the incident, but she soon detected that something was wrong, because during his next visit, I became afraid of him, grabbing onto Grandma's leg, not letting go until he left. She asked me in a gentle way, "Why are you afraid of that man?" When I did not respond, she asked me, "Did he touch you in a fresh way?" I said, "Yes." The next time he came over to visit, she confronted him about it, and told him to never come around again.

Another evening while left alone, I watched a television program about World War II and the Jewish Holocaust. I saw decaying bodies piled up in a pyramid; sunglasses, jewelry, even the gold that was taken from their teeth, all in a pile. I was horrified that this was going on somewhere in the world. No longer could I hold inside the insecurity and fear that so overwhelmed me. I began to cry day and night for my mother. I wanted to go home. Finally, Grandma could not tolerate me any more and packed my clothes.

It had been a year since I saw my family, with the exception of a few visits with Susan and Vicki. It was great to be heading home, and I looked forward to the homecoming. After an uneventful drive to Bay Shore, we pulled into the driveway of a little green three-bedroom house. Grandma stepped out of her car, grabbed my belongings, and literally threw my clothing on the front lawn. I remember the staring faces of my brothers and sisters, as I gladly got out of the back seat of her car. Not even this dramatic show on her part could diminish my happiness. I was home again. She did not enter the house, she only said a few harsh words and drove away.

I asked for Mom and was told that she was at work. Then I asked where Dad was, and was directed to the cellar. Rushing to the cellar to see the man I had not seen in two years, I received a cold welcome, as he told me not to come near him or speak to him. He was still bitter about Susan and Vicki escaping his judgement via their "convenient" marriages. I was not permitted to go near him until he discovered that Mom's hatred for me far outweighed his.

During Grandma's visits she expressed hatred towards me and was successful in coaxing Mom to mistreat me. Dad and I had one common bond, we hated her with a deep passion, and she hated us. Mom used to inflict beatings on me whenever she was around One day there was a carnival on the Bay Shore High School grounds down the street. The family was walking to it, and I ran to catch up with Dad and my siblings, when I heard Grandma say to Mom, "Look at her, she's running after her father, because she wants to go to bed with him. Do something, hija." Suddenly, I felt my hair being pulled from behind; it was Mom, uncontrollably punching me in the back with her fist.

Years later I found out that she also interrogated Susan in the same fashion about her eight-year-old daughter; convincing her that her daughter wanted to go to bed with her father. After months of Susan's abuse to her daughter, her husband finally caught on, and Grandma was forbidden to visit for a couple of years.

My childhood years were tainted by continued incidents of abuse such as these. The intensity of it all seemed to multiply when we moved to our next house. Dad's control of the family multiplied.

CHAPTER TWO

Dad's Tight-fisted Control

Looking back on those years in Bay Shore, I'm beginning to see how the resort atmosphere fitted Dad's style much better than city life. While manipulating and fully controlling our lives, he was able to enjoy doing what he liked: fishing, gardening, and artistic wall painting were among his favorite pursuits. His lust for boats, although he was not a proud owner of one, was high on his list. When he was in one of his infrequent good moods, he would tell us stories about how he had caught whales and great sharks while sailing the seas.

After living in Bay Shore for a couple of years, we moved to a less expensive place in a lower part of town. With this move, I received an onslaught of physical and mental torment. Even as a child, I sensed evil of every kind beginning to loom over our dwelling and our individual lives.

Dad's source of wisdom was his beloved sister Flora, the sorcerer. Although Flora hated Mom, she allowed her to accompany her brother during their periodic visits to Floral Park, where Flora lived in a huge, beautiful house.

The first thing he did upon settling in our new home was to take full control of everything. Family pictures were all collected and locked up in his locker (an antique armoire with a thick metal bar across it, with a lock) until the majority of them were expedited off the premises. No music was allowed to be heard, and God forbid if you got caught listening to music or dancing—you would qualify for a merciless whipping. We were allowed to watch television only when he was watching it and listen to music when he turned the radio on to listen to his tunes. To enforce this law, he switched the tubes in the radio so that during his absence we could not use it. When we had no music, Jonathan would sing for us, accompanied by banging on pots and pans as makeshift drums. We had a lot of fun, as he would use some of us children as background singers; Kelly had a great leading voice, and could impersonate Aretha Franklin, while Jonathan impersonated Elvis Presley and Smokey Robinson, and more.

When Dad took his spontaneous two months' vacation, James worked for days, switching the tubes around in the radio until it worked, and he became an expert at putting the tubes back where Dad had left them. When he was away, we danced and had a good time. Mom did not care what we did when he was not around, as though she were punishing him for not being there. Upon his return, the radio went off, James quickly put the tubes back, friends rushed upstairs, jumping into closets, and we ran around frantically, trying to make things look as though nothing was happening. The first thing he did when he entered the house, was to call each of our names like a drill sergeant, and whoever did not appear was in deep trouble.

Makeup, nail polish, stockings, perfume, and bras were confiscated. Anything that might enhance your femininity was forbidden—even if your breasts were fully developed, you were not allowed to wear a bra. Each night there was a room search, and if any of those items were found, they were removed. Mom and Kelly were the only ones permitted to wear bras and stockings.

Dad took control of the heat and hot water. In below-zero weather, on many days the heat and hot water were not turned on. Sometime we nailed a blanket to the entryway of the kitchen, lit the oven, and hung out in there. When you did take a bath, pots of water were boiled on the stove and poured into the tub in the hope that the water would not get cold before the rest of the water was heated. Dad, on the other hand, took a bath about once every three years; Mom chuckled at the historical event. When expecting company—his friends or family—the heat and the hot water were turned on. One of the reasons why we were not permitted to use much water was that we did not have linkage to the town sewage system, but rather a cesspool; and when it overflowed, it let off a horrible odor, alerting our neighbors that we had not paid the thirty-five dollars to have it cleaned out. What an embarrassment.

In contrast to the severe winters, summers were sultry and hot. One summer day, upon hearing the music of the ice cream truck, we children and other neighborhood kids ran out to the front yard as the truck stopped. We looked at Dad, who was working in the front yard, hoping desperately to get a treat; but instead we witnessed him purchasing ice cream for the other neighborhood children and not for us. He further embarrassed us by explaining to them that they were better than we were and that we were not worthy of receiving ice cream. The children made fun of us at school, telling other children what took place.

You were not permitted to look outside the window—an indication of signaling some guy to meet you later on—and private conversations were not allowed, unless he was included. If a whisper was heard, you were in trouble. Accepting gifts, even from your Sunday school teacher for learning your Bible verses, was forbidden. For instance, I received a bracelet containing a mustard seed as a reward for learning my Bible verses. It was immediately taken away from me, and a couple of years later given to Susan as a gift.

Having a permit to frequent the Bay Shore beach, and living within walking distance, we all walked to the beach about three times. We girls were not permitted to wear bathing suits, so we went in the ocean with our clothes on. Dad and the boys fished for blowfish, flounder, and other seafood. When James caught a blowfish, after the fish blew up like a ballon, he stomped on it, laughing.

Mom did try to feed us the best way she could, but the meals did not balance. There were times when we did not receive meat or fish with our meal, but Dad always had a large steak on his plate. He exercised his favoritism by slicing very thin pieces of steak and giving each person at the table a portion. The one who got the piece of meat first probably was going to meet him in the basement that night. He would take the fork with the piece of meat on it, extend it across the table and say, "Here, put this in your mouth." The anticipation of being offered a small piece of steak was highly intense, because if you did not receive a piece of meat, you were mocked by the other children.

Half of his meal was saved on the kitchen shelf for during the night, as he did not sleep much, needing to devise our torment for the following day as well as exercise his sex pleasures, and to insure its safety, he brought to our attention the fact that he had spit on it.

For every new gripe he created, we devised a new solution. At night the boys went on their scavenging expeditions. When sneaking out of the house got too tough for them, they tied sheets together, and climbed out of the second-story window. It was hilarious, because Dad's window was directly below the girls' window, where they quietly climbed down from, hoping their shadows would not be detected. Upon discovering that they were no longer in the house, he nailed shut every door and window to prevent them from re-entering. Next, he put out a decree that a judgment would be laid upon whoever let the boys back inside.

I waited up for the boys until the early morning hours, and twisted the nails on the basement window to let them back in. When Dad discovered that they were sleeping in their beds, frantically he lined us children up and used his scariest tactics in an attempt to find out who let them in. No one was motivated to tell out of fear, everyone knew the rule: "Keep your mouth shut, you know nothing." Besides, if you did tell, you risked getting a beating for not mentioning it sooner. When or if you did get ratted out, it was for personal vengeance. Such as the time when James, out of anger said, "Daddy, you know why Kelly has rollers in her hair? Because she cut her hair." Kelly had long beautiful hair below her waist, and she was not allowed to cut it. Mom agreed that she could, because the style for teenagers was teased hair with a flip to the neckline. So she wore her hair in rollers whenever he was around. (Her excuse to Mom was that the children at school was calling her a witch, because of her long hair; and was dipping her hair into their ink well, causing stains on her blouse.)

The thirteen of us developed a bond. Our purpose was to survive Dad's tight control, learning secret codes to signal each other on what to say, and how to act around him. Our craftiness increased day by day. It became a challenge to survive.

CHAPTER THREE

The Name of the Game Is Survival

With eleven children and two adults surviving on one income, Mom's meager salary as an attendant at the Pilgrim State Hospital (a mental institution), it was quite a job trying to provide the basic essentials. It did not take long to learn the name of the game was survival.

During Dad's absences, we were able to initiate our own survival program, which began in Jersey when Dad had abandoned the family.

Late one night, Jonathan and James took us children to Burry's cookie factory, where they stole large bags of cookies when the workers were not looking. They ran as fast as they could, with the rest of us tagging behind. The boys also hit the donut factory in similar fashion. We always had plenty of cookies and donuts to eat. Stealing the neighbor's bottled milk that was delivered in the early morning also started in Newark.

Upon moving to Bay Shore, our survival program grew to new proportions. There were plenty of woods around that grew wild flowers and blackberries, there were ponds filled with geese, and fresh water streams. Ma gave Sally and I big pots to put the blackberries and other berries in, for making pies. James went to the pond to collect goose eggs, and even brought a big goose home, as well as stealing rabbits from a neighbor who bred them. Another neighbor released his pigeons at a certain time of the day, and James learned how to call the pigeons to him; he'd change its band, branding them his.

The boys caught eels from the streams that had white sand around them—bait for catching fish. We called it the "Indian Reservation." How beautiful that place was.

When Mom was at work, I wore her clothing; high heels, jewelry and hat. Wildflowers grew in the woods across the street, and I sold them for a quarter to the elderly neighborhood women on the block. They called me "the actress", saying that they knew when I was coming down the street by the clicking of the high heels on the pavement.

Jonathan, James, and Peter robbed the big old abandoned houses near the ocean. Rumor had it that those houses were haunted. The boys brought home antique cans filled with gold and silver coins, and a can of hard rock candy. I remember a picture of a queen on the cans. James tried to entice us children to eat the candy and laughed at us for being too afraid to eat it after saying that the ghosts tried to prevent them from taking the treasures that were in the cellar by blowing out the candles each time they lit them. According to their story, the family's graves were also down there. The tales they told about their adventures were phenomenal!

We were beginning to get into all sorts of sinful acts to accommodate our existence.

At quite a young age, Sally and I also played our part by getting up early in the morning, collecting empty soda bottles from people's porches, and redeeming them for cash. We were subjected to everything and anybody. There was drugstore that caught on fire, and much of the merchandise was still in the store. We went home to tell Mom, who immediately followed us with the boys to the store to cash in.

On one of our scavenging hunts, like homeless children, dressed in rags, we came in contact with a very tall white man who sold used clothing and furniture. He told us that if we took our clothes off while he played with himself, he would give us a piece of used clothing. We both did, at separate times. He was true to his word, and gave us a piece of used clothing.

Mom bought a few fresh rolls to eat with her morning coffee before going to work, while we ate bread from the day-old bread store that cost one dollar for twelve loaves. During their middle of the night adventures, the boys discovered that the bakeries made early morning deliveries to the stores. They arrived before the store owners did to receive the goods. After learning their night routines, each child had to take a turn making the rounds while the others slept in.

Dad woke up one morning and saw us children, (even the smallest child), walking around eating a big Italian roll. In a rage, he demanded to know how we got those rolls; but to no avail—no one said a word.

About every three months, an ice cream truck parked a few blocks away; the driver was a weekend visitor to a neighbor. James stole gallons of ice cream from that truck; quietly he woke us up at about three o'clock in the morning, handing each of us a gallon of ice cream to eat. Although we were tired, we were happy to get the ice cream and ate until we were full and could not eat any more. James would force us to finish our gallon before Dad woke up, knowing that he would confiscate it—which he did, locking it up in the freezer. Even the refrigerator had a lock and chain around it. We were sent to school without lunch; we sat there watching the other children eat good lunches with a snack. I once asked a girl that if she had any corn chips left over, may I please have some. She at such a young age had compassion, and left some in the bag for me.

Joseph the youngest of the four brothers, did not engage in these ventures, although he did work selling eggs to our neighbors at a young age.

James and Peter sometimes took the boat to Fire Island from the Bay Shore marina to hang out there for the day, dropping their nets in the water, catching clams and eating them until they were full and bringing the rest home.

Peter found favor with Mr. Flynn, the owner of a high-society fish restaurant at the marina in Bay Shore and employed him to work there. Peter brought James and Joseph in to meet him, and he hired them, too. He explained to them that they could eat as much as they wanted, but not to touch the ice cream, which was imported from Italy.

James smuggled food out of the restaurant and brought it home for us to eat; stuffed clams and other exotic recipes were on the menu, and he would say, "This is rich people's food. Eat up!"

Recognizing Joseph industrious ways at such a young age, Mr. Flynn gave him a car, although Joseph was not old enough to drive. Dad kept the car for himself. Joseph cried so hard and we girls tried to comfort him. Joseph then built a bicycle from spare parts that he found and when the bike was finished, Dad ran over it with his car.

Ironically enough, dating back to Newark we all had to attend a Protestant church. In Bay Shore, it was the Church of the Nazarene, which provided a yellow bus to pick us up for church.

One Sunday, the pastor gave each person a paper box called an Alabaster Box. We were instructed to save our money in that box and return it to the church at the appointed time. My crafty little mind decided to let the neighborhood help us, and of course, Mom thought it was a good idea. Sally and I started knocking on doors a few blocks away from where we lived, asking people to please donate money to our church. People were very nice, and sometimes invited us in for a snack. We were respected for what we were doing, and no one took advantage of us. When our boxes got destroyed from the rain, we took a piece of paper and wrote on it "Alabaster Box" and taped it to a glass jar. We worked for many hours, until we could not walk anymore, collecting money. When we arrived home, we gave our jars to Mom and were never given a penny of that money for our personal use.

We did this for many months until one day a Jewish lady donated five dollars and then telephoned the pastor of our church to see if the money had been received. The following Sunday, Sally and I did not go home on the bus from church; we were escorted by the pastor, who first stopped at the woman's home to confirm that we were the right children. He then informed our parents of our sin, and they acted so surprised. In his presence, Mom questioned me as to what I did with the money. I replied, "I bought candy for the kids." Dad had to have known what we were doing, because we never got a beating for coming home late at night. The pastor left, and not a word was said to us by either party. The worst that happened to us was being made fun of by the boys; mostly James, as he said, "So, you got caught with your Alabaster Boxes, huh?" as he laughed.

To my astonishment, the Jewish woman wanted to meet with Mom, and before it was over, she hired her and Kelly to clean her house on the weekends. If Vicky was around, she also went along.

Mom sought a second job working on Main Street in Bay Shore, washing floors at an IBM keypunch school, which consisted of about four large classrooms and two lavatories. She took me along, walking about a mile from our home to Bay Shore High School to meet me; and from there, we walked to work. We earned three dollars per night. After a few nights, I informed her that she no longer needed to come along and that I could handle it alone. From school, I walked to work; and sometimes had to walk two and a half miles home at night in the rain, because Dad refused to pick me up. After a few months, my boss demanded that I come in on Saturday to wax the floors, without pay. I told him that I did not work for free, thereby ending my employment. With the money that I had saved, I bought our first washing machine with rollers to ring out the clothes; being careful not to let anyone's fingers get caught in the rollers.

Susan stole money from her husband's pockets while he was asleep; Vicky dated other men, such as her boss and her father-in-law for extra cash, which they gave to Mom during their weekend visits.

CHAPTER FOUR

Holiday Celebrations

Every holiday, Dad provoked an argument with Mom, giving him an excuse to go and live with his other wife and four children or to be with his two friends whom he dated. Tommy was a homosexual and Ernie was bi-sexual who had a wife and three children. She deeply sobbed as he left, dressed in expensive attire: a brown business suit, dress shirt, tie, brown leather shoes, brown hat, and a purple long coat with fur around the collar. We tried to comfort her as best we could, but his departure was disturbing. She knew where he was going, but we did not.

We always knew when he was leaving, by the amount of hours he spent occupying the bathroom, coloring his hair jet black and trying to hand wash the months of stench off his body.

Christmas

Christmas was the worst time of the year, especially having to attend church on that day, wearing hand-me-down clothes from other church members. We were made fun of by our classmates. "Hey, she is wearing my dress!" one girl said about me to the other children.

The season only seemed to enhance the contrast between our deprived, abused existence and the well-being that permeated the other families in the church. Children attended church accompanied by their parents, who loved and dressed them in new holiday attire.

Christmas also meant charity to our family. The used toys that no one wanted anymore were donated to us by the church and other community organizations. When we did receive new toys, they were taken away from us while we were sleeping and given to Dad's other children in the city.

One Christmas morning I received a new Betsy McCall doll that had been donated to me; it was the best gift I ever received as a child. She had ice skates and several changes of clothing. Quickly, I went outside to play in the snow, as Dad watched through the window, observing how much fun I was having. That was the last time I ever saw her.

That same Christmas, Sally and I each received a used, three-foot-tall Patty Play Pal doll donated by my elementary school teacher, who sent me home from school, stating that I was no longer fit to be around the other children, due to my unkept appearance—dirty clothes, uncombed hair, and unbathed. She took the initiative to visit our home, only to discover the degree of neglect there, which motivated her to make that donation. But all toys were abolished from the house.

If you think going to church on Christmas Day wearing used clothing was an issue, returning to school from a two-week Christmas vacation was even worse. That was when everyone sported their new clothing.

In my first year of high school, Vicki bought me Christmas gifts, which consisted of a new dress, shoes, a notebook, pens, and pencils. The night before our first day back to school, Dad confiscated those items, causing me to return to Bay Shore high wearing torn sneakers and rags. I was made fun of, and also threatened by a boy not to get on the school bus home.

About the age of fifteen, Kelly, the "princess" of the family, finally decided to help. Kelly, Sally, and I took the four younger girls to the shopping mall during the Christmas rush, Tonya and Cindy in the stroller, Dorothy and Latashha holding onto the sides of the stroller, and Sally nearby. During our shopping spree, clerks volunteered to accommodate us, fitting the girls into clothes and shoes; and when no one was looking, we quickly stuck those items underneath the baby's blanket and walked out of the store. The girls were dressed in new attire for Christmas, and Mom was pleased when we showed her the things that we got.

Christmas trees and decorations of any kind were abolished. During one of Dad's long absences, Joseph, about ten years old then, went out on South Spur drive and cut down a pine tree and brought it home. Excitement arose, and us girls made Christmas ornaments out of colored paper and hung them on the tree. On Christmas Day, Dad came home and threw the tree out in the yard.

Ma was always trying to get me to wear the clothes and sneakers she stole from the Pilgrim State Hospital. I did not want to wear them, knowing that everyone recognized those clothes, because almost every parent in the surrounding neighborhoods worked at that hospital, including Jonathan and his new bride.

Unlike most Christmas holidays, Mom bought gifts for the children, and I searched through the bags to see what was bought for me. She said, "I didn't buy you anything, because you are smart and understand." That was more than I could bare, I started yelling at her with a loud voice, until Dad came out of his room inquiring as to why I was yelling. Not changing my tone, I told him that she did not buy me a gift, but bought everyone else one. He demanded that she go back to the store to buy me a gift, and do not return without one. I went with her to pick out what I wanted.

Thanksgiving

Not all holiday memories were unhappy ones. A few months earlier, when I was fourteen, I ran away from home. I missed the family, and on Thanksgiving day I sneaked back to see Mom and the other children. With the tablecloth covering the table, I was able to hide without being seen. Dinner had not yet been served, as my brothers and sisters walked through the dark dinning room socializing with me while I remained underneath the table. Dad got wise to my game, and invited me to dine with the family.

He proceeded to give a very long prayer before dinner, making mention of me, his "prodigal" daughter. After several minutes of that, everyone became restless, and started making secret jokes about him, by kicking and pinching each other.

He caught Sally laughing, and jumped up across the table to hit her, when a board fell down from the wall, hitting him on the head and almost knocking him out. That Thanksgiving day was a memorable one, and was talked about for some time.

He was happy that I was there and allowed me to get drunk. As I tried to give the dog a turkey leg to eat, Mom comically screamed, "No, don't give the turkey leg to the dog!" Everyone was happy that day, including Susan and Vicki (and their families), because the family was all together.

Halloween

Halloween was never a time of pressure. We were allowed to collect as much candy as we wanted to. Sometimes we trick-or-treated early, so that Mom could have candy to pass out to the neighborhood children.

After collecting candy for several hours, when we arrived back home with our bags filled with all sorts of goodies, Dad searched our bags for the "nickel" bars (large candy bars), especially the chocolate ones, and placed them in his locker. When the candy became old and wormy, he brought them out and gave them to us to eat. After this experience, we learned to hide as many nickel bars as possible before he got into our bags.

James and Peter came home with several bags of candy that they said they had stolen from other children. The thought of them stealing candy from other children made me angry.

One Halloween when Dad was not home, I borrowed his good suit, shirt, shoes, and hat as a costume and left the house in the rain to trick or treat. When I arrived home, the hat and suit were sopping wet, and the shoes were covered with mud. I took everything off, and neatly put each item back in the closet. Upon his return a few days later he opened his closet door and let out a high-pitched shriek. He came out of his room, holding up the pair of muddy shoes, saying, in his British accent, "Be Jesus Christ, look what happened to me kiss-me-ass shoes! Who the hell did this to my shoes?" Everyone restrained themselves from bursting out laughing. When he was out of hearing range, we all had a good laugh, including Mom.

I remember those rare occasions when he left his den unlocked to use the bathroom. I quickly ravaged through the pockets of his clothes for money and did not come out empty-handed, nor was I ever caught.

Easter

One Easter, an organization donated a very large basket filled with candy. Kelly and I colored eggs the night before Easter to prepare for the following day's egg hunt after church for our siblings. Susan and Vicki also brought colored eggs and candy treats.

Birthday Time

By this time, you should know that birthday parties were not permitted.

My twelfth birthday was approaching, and Dad had not been around for weeks. I begged Mom to let me have some friends over and have a party, and she consented. We had our friends over, and the party was going great! We were dancing and popping balloons, when suddenly Dad arrived. He walked in and asked, "What the hell is going on?" He turned the record player off and kicked everyone outside into the freezing November rain. By that point, I was getting to the end of my rope with him and everyone else in the family.

Another year, for the first time that I could remember, Mom and Kelly decided to bake a birthday cake for him. He came out in disgust, laughed and said, "You fools, all these years you have been celebrating my birthday on the wrong day." He looked at me and said, "They don't even know when I was born."

CHAPTER FIVE

Marketing: The Ups and Downs

When Dad was away, Mom had no transportation, nor did she know how to drive; and since I had to be home for the family's needs, I was usually the one who had to walk to the market to do the grocery shopping. I did not mind, as it gave me an opportunity to get out of the house. She gave me a list of the few things to buy, and after paying for them, I took extra big bags from the register and went back through the store, filling up bags with food. One time, a man who was not an employee, after seeing what I was doing, told me that I better put those things back. I put a few things back, and then proceeded to push the shopping cart a mile or so home. Mom was always happy when I got home safe with the goods.

James and Peter never wanted to do the shopping, although they were the only ones who had bicycles, which they built from parts they found or stole, and they did not allow anyone to ride them. I borrowed them any time I had a chance, to shop for Mom. Once their bikes were resting against the front of the house, so I went inside to ask if she needed anything from the store. She reached into her bra and handed me a dollar for twelve loaves of bread, from the store that was about two miles away. I made it there safely, but on the way home, I went flying in the air along with twelve loaves of bread. They had decided to teach me a lesson by removing the screws from the front wheel; it came apart while I was riding.

They waited for me to come home so that they could enjoy a good laugh. I arrived with bruises and cuts; I'd left the bike where it fell apart. Months later, I forgot about that incident, and took the bicycle again, this time with Dorothy on the handlebars. Going down a hill very fast, the same thing happened, and I was seriously injured, resulting in a scar I have on my knee until this day. Dorothy was injured, too, but not severely, as she landed on top of bushes.

Although our neighborhood was predominately black, it was interesting how some white children from outside our development managed to find their way inside our home. There was an unattractive boy nicknamed Peanut, who was fond of Kelly. We girls put a sheet over their heads while they sat and kissed. When the kissing was over, he went to the supermarket and filled up a couple of big brown bags with a pound of Hersey chocolate candy bars, and brought them home to us. Usually, James would not allow any guy around us girls, but he liked Peanut because he was not afraid to steal from the supermarket.

Our family did not qualify for welfare, but the government did, at a later date, provide us with "surplus" food—food that was no longer stored because it had passed its expiration date. Dad took Mom to a field where the food was being distributed. The needy families were allotted food according to the number of people in their family. Sometimes in below-zero weather, she was dropped off to stand in line for many hours while he remained in the heated car or returned home until he thought she was ready to be picked up. Anticipating her arrival, I heated the oven. She entered the house with tears in her eyes because her hands and feet were frostbitten due to lack of proper clothing. After standing in front of the oven until she was warm, she began to open the boxes to show us the cheese, butter, flour, canned meat, and other foods she had acquired. Dad boldly entered the kitchen, put the perishable food in the locked refrigerator, and took the rest to a locked room.

The government abolished the surplus food program, and replaced it with food stamps. Going to the supermarket or anywhere else, outside of taking her to work (and even sometimes that) was always a big ordeal for Dad. When he did agree to take us to the market, he left us there for several hours. If the store closed while we were waiting, we waited in the night at a deserted tiny shopping mall.

One day the food stamps arrived but we had no way of getting to the market other than hitch-hiking, which we did often, as there were no public buses to take you anywhere. Jonathan arrived in the middle of the night, leaving his car parked in the driveway. At mid-afternoon, while he was still asleep, Kelly suggested we sneak the key out of his pocket and go food shopping. Mom thought that was a great idea. Kelly, Mom, and I with child got into the car and left. Although Kelly was about twenty years old, she did not know how to drive very well. We coached her all the way from Brentwood to Bay Shore. When we arrived, we parked far away from the other cars, only to discover, when our shopping was finished, that there were cars parked all around our car. Kelly tried to back out, and hit the car behind us, then she tried to turn, and hit another car. Before we got out of the parking lot, she hit about five parked cars. Mom said, "Hurry, let's get out of here!"

When we arrived home, we quietly put the food away, and Kelly returned the key. Upon discovering the condition of his car, Jonathan panicked, wanting to know what had happened to it. Each dent had a different color of paint. Frantically, he asked Ma, "What happened to my car?" She said in a stern voice, "Don't ask me nothing. I know nothing!" Of course no one knew anything about the car. Afterwards, we all had a good laugh.

CHAPTER SIX

Incest and Its Effects

Dad and Girls

After Mom was dropped off at work, Kelly went to bed, where she remained until late afternoon, shortly before Ma's arrival. While washing the dishes, Dad said to me "Shhhh, Kelly Is sleeping, and I don't want you to wake her up." While she was asleep, during summer vacation, he was sexually molesting the other girls and boys.

One day, Sally informed Mom about Dad's sexual advances towards her. Mom confronted him about the accusation in the presence of family members. Outraged, Dad began to assault Sally. and forced her to say that it was a lie. I asked, "Mom, why didn't you do something to help her?" She said, "Don't tell me anything and you won't get a beating." Another time she said, "If you girls did'nt like it, he would'n do it." Soon after that, everyone got the picture: "put out or shut up." She knew exactly who he was having perverted sex with,and when; she got her kicks from being the "peeping Mom," watching through the dark shadows and bragging to other people how James was his favorite one.

To further justify his right, Dad referred to the Bible story of Lot having sex with his two daughters. He said it must be okay or it would not be in the Bible; then he directed our attention to the passage that said, "Children, obey your parents in all things, for this is well pleasing to the Lord."

Dad's beating's were mean. He used a wide leather belt that was cut into six strips (a razor strap) so that each lash was equivalent to six, ensuring that you received welts, bruises, and sometimes blood. I experienced that beating, and when it was over I ran upstairs to my room, where I was greeted by James, a mean-spirited person who interrogated and mocked me. His hatred toward me was deep. "Did it feel good? I bet it tickles, huh? Can you describe what your body is going through right now? I loved the way you were screaming after each lash. C'mon, cry. I want to see you cry some more." Then he would imitate my performance when I was being whipped.

I was spared greatly from Dad's, rape. although no one escaped totally. I graduated from the room upstairs shared by the other girls, to Kelly's small bedroom on the first floor next to our parents' room. Kelly and I slept in the same single bed.

In the middle of the night, he crept into our bed and started rubbing my vagina, waking me up; then he heard Mom walking by, jumped up, and ran out the room.

Even at a young age, it was a never ending battle between Dad and me, with this sex thing; his forcefully grabbing me, trying to put his tongue in my mouth. When I broke away from his grip, I said, "You are a sick man and you need help." He laughed. Other times he approached me like a little boy, begging for a kiss; when I turned him down, he said, "You don't love your daddy" and I said, "I do love you, but not that way." When my breasts began to develop, it got worse. He would take me into the den and try to explain to me that if I let him suck my breasts, they would grow bigger.

Since he could not get an "arrangement" with me, he was going to make my life as difficult as possible. He openly disgraced me in front of Mom, and the entire family, by forcing me to sit on a stool in the living room naked from my waist up while he pretended to remove a mole that I have in the middle of my chest. After about ten minutes, he left, ordering me not to move until he got back—which was about two hours later. James entered the house and there I was with my breasts exposed; he immediately turned his head and walked away. He knew that if I had given way in secret like the rest of them, I would not have been openly exposed.

Dad stopped his sex advances and I became the housekeeper, which was not an easy job. Waking up at five o'clock in the morning to bake biscuits and corn bread for breakfast, combing the girls' hair and dressing them for school, ironing Mom's uniform for work, waking the boys up (and risking a beating), and then getting myself ready for school. In the evening: cleaning the house, cooking dinner, scrubbing clothes in the tub, on a wash board; which sometimes meant frostbitten fingers in the winter from hanging clothes on the line and athlete's fingers in the summer from the boys' socks. On the weekends I groomed Kelly for hours, styling her very long hair and painting her nails. Sometimes I got a beating from her for not doing an excellent job.

Susan came back, asking for Dad's forgiveness so that she could visit with Mom and the rest of the family. He consented with open arms, and the romance began again. When she got tired of it, she told her husband, who then stopped the weekend visits, and instead visited Mom on her job at the hospital. Mom cared less about Susan's company. Her interest was in the money, free lunches, and whatever else was given to her from Susan, who played the role of an innocent little girl, enticing her husband to buy her jewelry and other gifts, which she passed on to Mom.

Eventually, Susan caught on to Ma's lack of interest in her and was at our doorstep again, asking for Dad's pardon. He never refused any of us children to enter the "house of hell." This time there was to be no squealing from Susan, as the romancing took place in his den behind the locked door.

One weekend when Susan, Vicki, and their families arrived to visit us, Sally told everyone that she was having sex with Dad. Everyone was astonished, not at the accusation, but the admitting of it. It was a well kept "secret" that no one ever talked about. "How else was I supposed to get school clothes and other necessities, if I did not sleep with him?" she said.

Vicki, on the other hand, had a thing going on with Dad, and he was certainly no threat to her; if anything, he was a challenge.

One day during my weekend visit, he opened his locker and handed me a pornographic photo album of Vicki—married and a mother at that time—posing in different positions totally nude. He said, "Look at this nasty bitch. She gave this to me." I could not believe my eyes.

Brother and Sisters

There were occasions when my parents left for the weekend, always taking Kelly and leaving me behind to care for the two babies and the other children. Being twelve years old, I suffered deep pain from never being permitted to go along.

Sometimes James would be in the house, waiting to terrorize me. He did not do this to anyone else but me. I received many brutal beatings and he sexual assaulted me; he was very strong, and I weighed only eighty-five pounds.

During one of their weekend trips, James and Peter held me down at the bottom of the stairs, a few feet away from the front entrance. They took my underwear off and directed Joseph (who was still a baby) to put his penis in me.

Another time James picked me up and was carrying me to Mom's bedroom as I screamed, "Put me down! Let me go!" and tried to get away from him. Kelly and the younger girls started beating him with garbage, throwing bottles and cans at him until he had to let me go.

James's beatings were sometimes worse than Dad's. One time he threw me down a flight of stairs and then proceeded to kick me in the stomach, causing my menstrual blood to soak through my clothing.

Another time, when he discovered that I was down the street visiting a girlfriend, he met me on the way home, grabbed me by my hair, and dragged me down the street. At home, he beat me with his fists. Our siblings were upset because they loved me and relied on me for everything (except for sally, who had a hidden jealously). When Mom and Dad arrived home and were informed of these events, they simple ignored it. The abuse became so frequent that it appeared to be normal, and James began beating me in front of the weekend family visitors.

One day he began to beat me in the living room where Dad sat reading the newspaper. The blows were steady, and I fell on the floor at Dad's feet. When I screamed for help, he put the newspaper high up, covering his face, as if to say, "I do not see that." James then took the metal bar from his locker and struck me a few times with it. Susan and Vicki began to scream, "Please stop! Dad, do something!" They ran into the kitchen. "Mom, please make him stop!" Mom shook her head no.

When the beating was over, I was petrified. I had reached my end. Murder was in my heart and I wanted to kill James.

Later, I was in the kitchen alone with Vicki, crying my heart out. I said to her, "I swear to God, I'm going to scald him with boiling hot water. I'm going to pour it on him when he is sleeping." Vicki said no, "Here is what you do, take a knife and put it on the stove until it turns red, then stick it on his ass."

I stayed awake, pretending to be asleep, waiting until the whole family retired. At around two o'clock in the morning, I got up, took a large, wide knife, and put in on the stove until it turned red. Then I went upstairs to the boys' room, pulled James's underwear down, and stuck the knife on his buttock. He howled, and immediately went downstairs to show Dad what I had done to him. The whole household was alarmed, as I waited on the stairs to hear the reaction. But there was none. Only silence. I expected screams, yelling, or possibly a beating, but there was only silence. I wonder to this day what was said in that room.

I went to sleep, and the following morning there was no mention or confrontation. It was as though it never happened. The only time it was ever mentioned, was when Mom found it so comical that James had to go to court a week later for some crime he had committed. She laughed as she was telling someone how the judge said to him, "Sit down," he did not. Angrily, the judge said, "Sit down." Painfully, James sat down. Mom found that so funny, as she said, "Nancy took a knife and burned his ass." I never received another beating or any harassment from him again. I realized many years later that he was instructed by my parents to abuse me. After that incident, he never abused me again, nor did I ever get a beating from anyone after that except Dad, when I lived at home.

The only thing James did a couple of times was to wake me up, saying in a soft voice, "Nancy, wake up." When I opened my eyes, there was the iron a few inches away from my face, and I screamed. He would laugh and quickly run away. The iron was cold.

Jonathan was a quiet, gentle-spirited person although one day he said to me that he would give me candy if I let him have sex with me. That did not happen. He was not into beating people. Vicki, on the other hand, wanted him for her part-time lover.

When the family moved to Bay Shore, it was Jonathan's responsibility to take care of the children and the household, which he did as best he could. Upon Mom's arrival, he left, and returned in the middle of the night. A few years later, he joined the navy with the expectation of changing his life. He discovered a few months later that his underage girlfriend Linda was having his baby. The child had to be given up until they got married. Mom and Dad got together with the baby's grandparents and arranged for Vicki to care for the child until the couple got married, at which point she would return the baby to them. After the wedding, Vicki refused to return the child. Years later, Jonathan revealed that our parents were aware of how Vicki pleaded with him to have sex with her, and when he refused, she became treacherous towards him.

In-laws

It was not long before the in-laws entered the incest scene. Vicki married a pervert who sexually molested Sally and myself.

By some miracle, she convinced Dad to let me stay with her for a month, during my summer vacation. I was then introduced to evil acts, and a new method of child molestation. This time it was not by threat, beatings, or by force—it was by kindness and gentleness, something I was not accustomed to, as he was aware of.

During my stay with them, Vicki dated other men, including her father-in-law in the evening, leaving me along with her husband and toddler. Her husband Palaam undressed me and proceeded to have sexual intercourse with me. Another time, I fell asleep with my clothes on, and in the morning, after realizing that I was in my pajamas, I thanked Vicki for changing me. She immediately exploded, because she knew it was her husband who had undressed me, and he probably did more than that. Once had sex with me upstairs in our house, and I noticed him signaling James to keep guard; which tells me this has been going on for a while, he and James molesting the girls.

Not long after that, Vicki fell in love with a high-school boy named Ray and soon divorced Palaam to marry him. She was unaware that Ray also was a victim of perverted child molestation by his father Luis. She informed her mother-in-law about her affair with her husband, causing them to divorce. A few months after her second wedding, she got caught having sex with Ray's brother Ricky, who was not retarded, but slow. Her in-laws gave her a beating. She told me, "Nancy, they beat the shit out of me, but I got some licks in, too." Everyone in the family talked about her beating.

When things settled down, Vicki allowed her two sons—Jonathan's son Vincent and her first born Ronald—to spend the weekends with her new in-laws. When the day came, they cried, "No, Mommy, please don't let us go there." She asked, "Why not?" They said, "Grandpa has been having sex with us. I don't want to go there anymore." While Vicki explained this to me, Ronald said, "I was glad she found out, my booty was getting sore." Vicki said, "We went to his house, tied him up, stripped him naked, and stuck a broomstick up his rectum."

During one of my weekend visits, I heard some voices in the early morning hours. I quietly walked down the stairs to peek at whoever was there. I saw Mom and Dad talking to Vicki at the back door. They said to her, "You better not ever come around here making accusations like that again, or you will never be allowed here again." Then I saw Kelly and Vicki's husband Ray appear. Mom quietly told.Kelly, "You two better leave and do not let Vicki see you two together." I never told anyone what I saw and heard until now.

Brother and Wives

As a married woman, I found it quite comical to learn that James and Jonathan were wife-swapping. James married a Polish–Italian woman, and Jonathan married an Italian. It was humorous to see how Linda and Karen went along with this ludicrous game.

During my short five-month stay at the house, fights broke out between the two men, each proclaiming how the other had violated his wife. When they could not reach an agreement, broomsticks went flying, wives went screaming and running. One locked herself in the bathroom; doors were knocked down, and we all stood there laughing, as Mom screamed about the place being destroyed. Jonathan ran upstairs and barricaded the door so that James could not enter, so he ran to the small bathroom downstairs where Jonathan's wife had locked herself in. He took the broom stick and shoved it through the thin wooden door, leaving a hole. Afterwards, he put his eye to the hole, and said, sweetly, "Hello in there. I see you." Laughing, he said, "Are you scared? I'm coming to get you." He laughed even harder. All of us laughed, except for Mom, because the house was being destroyed.

Cousins

I saw Susan (married with children) kissing our cousin Frank on the mouth during one of their visits to Aunt Flora's while her husband Jose was in the kitchen still saying his good-byes. Kelly witnessed it, too, although she did not care; she dated our half-cousin Johnny a few times.

CHAPTER SEVEN

Drugs, Busts, Smoking, and Boozing It Up

My first encounter with cigarette smoke was when I was about six years old. Susan was sitting in the dark, looking out the window, probably waiting for a signal from her boyfriend, and weeping because she was not able to sneak out that night. She asked me to secretly get a cigarette out of Mom's purse for her, which I did. She gave me a couple of puffs from the cigarette.

Seven years later, I became a cigarette smoker, being the only person in the family except for Dad who was allowed to smoke openly in the house, or smoke at all. Because of my heavy duties, he kept me well supplied with cigarettes; when he could not afford to buy them, he bought tobacco and we rolled our own cigarettes on his little machine. If I managed to upset him, which was not hard to do, one of my punishments was that the privilege of smoking was taken away for a week.

One day, Mom, Kelly, and I had decided to treat ourselves to a cigarette in the privacy of the only little bathroom in the house, barely big enough for us three to fit in, when we heard screams from the other children, warning us that Dad had arrived. Quickly, we ran out of the bathroom and found him standing there. Not only was it bad enough to get caught socializing in the bathroom behind a closed door, but to see a mass of cigarette smoke pouring out from the bathroom won the prize. His voice took a high pitch, as usual when he was angry, and he said, "Look at the smoke!" Ma became hostile and answered him, "There is no cigarette smoke coming out from this bathroom." Then she called him every kind of liar that she could think of. He lost that battle.

Obsessed with catching us in the act, periodically he would change cars; and if the engine was loud enough to be heard, he parked down the street and walked home, hoping not to be detected, so that he could peep in the window and observe us for a while, before making his presence known.

One particular time, Ma felt comfortable enough to smoke openly in the kitchen, when he sneaked into the house and caught her. Swiftly he tried to slap the cigarette out of her mouth; but instead, slapped her face. She became so aroused she punched him in the eye, causing it to turn black and blue. He wore sunglasses until the bruise went away, while we laughed at the lies he told the neighbors about his eye.

Alcohol

Dad had quite a garden, with vegetables, herbs, and grapes, which he converted into moonshine wine. He took the grapes and put them through a metal grinder, then into a cloth and squeezed out the juice. The juice was then put into four crock pots kept in the cellar, with pounds of sugar and plenty of yeast. When the fermenting process was completed, it was transferred into glass bottles, leaving the maggots at the bottom of the crock to be strained later. Sometimes these pots would explode. At the age of nine, I told the guests not to drink the wine because there were maggots in it, which made Dad very angry.

When he had his friends or family over, the atmosphere was completely changed, almost like a rehearsed performance: Ma in the kitchen cooking, Dad dressed in his Sunday best, serving the finest cocktails money could buy, with a smile on his face that seemed to hurt him after a while as he sweated, wiping the makeup from his brow or possibly the black dye from his newly colored hair. If we entered the room, he gave us such a fierce look, that one would think he had little machine guns planted in his eyes, ready to shoot at a moment's notice. We were taught, "Children should be seen, not heard." If you ever entered his domain, you better have a good excuse, and the only time I was called in was to empty an ashtray or clean up some spill.

One evening while Dad was entertaining company, Kelly and I went to our little room, a few feet away, and smoked a cigarette. Afterwards, we played a game that was common in our household, balancing each other, in the air by our feet. One person would put their feet on the other's stomach, holding hands, as you were lifted. The laughter and excitement brought Dad around to investigate—and the smoke came pouring out of the room. He put on quite a performance for the quests, requesting them to enter our room to verify the smoke; when Mom made her way to the front of the crowd she shouted, "This cigarette smoke is not from this room. The smoke is coming from the guest smoking in the living room!" That shut him up, and the guests, too, who did not like her anyway.

Oh, how I loved those long good-byes in front of the house, as I waited patiently with my empty glasses, to fill it up, with whatever kind of booze left there until being locked up again, until the next time. Kelly was standing by to help transfer the glasses upstairs, where our party began later on.

During my weekend visits, when I was not yet old enough to purchase liquor, I gave Mom money to purchase about eight bottles of liquor from the corner store to accommodate my weekend stay, for myself and anyone else who wanted to join in on my upstairs party. Every word during the party was spoken in a whisper, and I wonder if we enjoyed it better that way, knowing we had a demonic bomb downstairs waiting to explode at any moment. He was getting up there in age, though, and had had a couple of heart attacks, so he did not scare us too much anymore.

One morning Dad came upstairs snooping around, searching the closets, checking underneath the beds for some kind of evidence; when he opened the cubby hole, bingo! He found weeks of wine and tango bottles stashed in there, and let out a scream for Ma in such a voice that one would have thought he'd found a corpse. Again, no one "knew anything" about those bottles, and Ma gave him such a ridiculous excuse, it only made him more angry.

Drugs

Mom was employed long enough to gain seniority,and she smuggled out merchandise such as clothing, pajamas, pillowcases, sheets, blankets, milk, ice cream, toothpaste, sneakers, and drugs.

The first time I recall drugs entering the house, it was for me. I was given Darvon and Valium at the age of eleven to calm my nerves. The pressure of everything that was going on, and the lack of understanding, became too much for me to bear. I began to freak out with relentless screams, pulling out my eyebrows, eyelashes, and hair. These were indications of a nervous breakdown. James composed bad songs about me, which were sung by family members, provoking me into a rage. Talk of putting me in a mental institution often came up, and became a family joke, making it even worse. When I went into a fit, and there was no drug to help me, Mom told the boys to take me upstairs and lock me in the closet and I cried, begged, and screamed to be let out.

One day Dad came home and heard me. He said, "Why is Nancy screaming?" Ma answered, "Because I had the boys lock her in the closet." He said, "Well, you have them unlock her from the closet." When I came out, I was trembling and crying. He then took me into his bedroom and put me in bed, telling Mom, "Don't you enter this room while she is in here." He rubbed my back until I fell asleep.

Jonathan, being heartbroken over not having his son, and with the pressures he and his new bride endured, turned to drugs. They became heroin hype junkies and soon James and Peter joined them. Sally moved out in her early teens, and followed in their footsteps. A few years later, when James went to prison, his wife also went to drugs.

When the boys could not get a fix, they experienced pain and agony, waiting for Mom to arrive with the drug to calm them down. Most of the time, James was the one suffering for a fix, while Jonathan and Peter enjoyed watching him doubled over, squirming and pleading for help. Feeling sorry for James, I begged them to give him a fix. Peter said, "If we give him a fix, he is going to beat us up and take our dope." Jonathan said that he was a ruthless animal and that it was nice to see him not so tough for a change. After he pleaded with them, they said, "Watch this." They got the cooker out, (a bottle cap or a spoon), cooked the heroin, and sucked it up in a hypodermic syringe, tied a string around James's arm, and injected him with the heroin. A few minutes later, James started punching Jonathan and Peter, asking them why they made him wait so long—and where is the rest of the dope? Peter said, "See, what did I tell you, Nancy?" Jonathan said to James, "See, I should have let you die. The next time, I will." Those boys always had hepatitis, walking around with yellow eyes from using each other's dirty needle. I have seen them overdose, laying there stiff, cold and blue, when immediately another family member would inject salt and water into their veins and afterward give mouth to mouth resuscitation to bring them back to life. It always worked.

Although Jonathan and James were married to very nice girls, they lived more often at home than with their wives, who still lived with their parents. Jonathan, after his three-year prison term for deserting the navy, married the woman he loved; on the other hand, James got his girlfriend Karen pregnant and her New York City bouncer father forced him to marry her. This Polish man, huge in size and a no-nonsense person, came a few times looking for James, who, whenever he saw his car, ran out the back door. After a few times, he got busted, and was forced to get married.

1968, we moved from Bay Shore to Central Islip, and a year later to Brentwood. We were already crime-oriented, and the drug scene now caused the family to escalate their illegal activities to support their addictions by robbing stores and homes, breaking into cars, and pushing drugs.

One evening, an elderly couple, neighbors who lived a few houses away, were visiting—while Kelly and the boys robbed their home. For the first time I saw Dad really angry about the crime that was committed against our neighbors.

James became so insane that the police no longer frightened him much. Stopped for a traffic violation, he pulled the gun from the officer's holster and commanded him to run, saying, "I will count to ten, and if you are still in my face, I will shoot you."

Jonathan, James and Peter started selling "heroin". Jonathan bought the drugs in Harlem and took it to Long Island to use and . My husband Frank and I (who was presently living at home, due to my pregnancy), went with Jonathan to pick up the drugs. He left us in the car. We became afraid and hid on the floor of the car . About one o'clock a.m., we got tired of waiting and Frank went in search for him and found Jonathan in a bar. The dealers got scared and said, "Hey, you brought the man here. No deal." Jonathan said, "No, he's not the man, he's my brother-in-law."

It was not long before the police set up a sting operation. A narc, acting the part of a homeless junkie, found favor with the boys and became their friend. For approximately six months, they shot up heroin together; he slept in my parents' home and ate at our table. After learning all the stops and dealers, the big bust took place. The narcotic agents and police were closing in. The narc pointed Jonathan out, as Mom cried, "The bastard ate here, slept here, and even had the audacity to call me Mom." It was considered one of the biggest drug busts in the history of Long Island.

Dad almost had a heart attack when the police forced him to unlock his den and his locker that was loaded with years of stolen goods, even some of the toys that he'd taken away from us as little children.

The cops came back in the middle of the night to harass us, sometimes busting down the door and lining everyone against the wall, including the children and grandchildren. When they came looking for Peter, I took him to the basement and dressed him in my clothes, stuffed socks in his shirt for breasts, and put Mom's wig on his head. Dad got a charge out of that, and so did everyone else. The next time they came looking for him, Mom and Dad stayed locked in their room, scared. I boldly answered the door. "Can I help you?" They said they were looking for Peter. I made a joke about it and then I said, "Get the hell out of here, and don't come back without a warrant!" They said, "Okay, we'll get him on his job at the restaurant." When they left, I quickly ran to the corner telephone booth and phoned the restaurant, warning Peter that the police were on their way to get him. He immediately ran out the back door. Mr.Flynn reserved his position for many months, until he was released from jail. His love for my brothers was unconditional.

Making it on my own, I got high from smoking marijuana and experimented with hash, acid, mescaline, and orange sunshine that made you hallucinate, thinking that you are in another world. The most horrible experience.

CHAPTER EIGHT

Making It on My Own

Harsh, degrading words were always used on us children, such as, "You'll never amount to anything, you're not fit to breathe the air, you're not worthy of the ground you walk on, you should have died in your mother's belly," and more. When we reached adolescence, "You'll be nothing but whores and prostitutes; society will never accept you." The boys were addressed as "faggots" and "queers." I cringed at these words, saying to myself, "One day I will prove this man wrong." He called Mom a "whore master," and she in return called him dirty names.

Entering our teenage years, we were not permitted to visit a school friend, or if asked out by their parent's to visit a drive-in movie, the answer was always no. Sometimes I would ask, hoping maybe one time Dad would say yes. No matter what the situation was, it was almost impossible to get permission to go anywhere while he was there. A few times he did allow us to go roller skating with the church.

His reasoning was that it was not good to have friends. He said to me, "The president of the United States has a plan to collect all the niggers and put them into huge ovens, and bake them; the same way Hitler did the Jews. He's just waiting until he's fed up with them." (Smiling as he said this.) He also said that the Puerto

Rican people were the lowest forms of human beings and were equal to animals (Ma stood by, agreeing). Then he said that white people were trash and that we should not associate with them. That basically eliminated everyone outside the family. Interestingly, he had dead straight hair and his skin was dark.

Living in a predominately black neighborhood, it was hard not to respond to a teenager you went to school with and who lived in your neighborhood. If you did, your face was slapped when you got home; and when you did not respond, you were chastised at school.

One day he threatened me while I stood at the top of the stairs. He ran up a few steps, as a gesture for me to run and hide under the bed in fear; only I did not move. He ran up a few more stairs, and I stood there looking him in his eyes. Then he ran all the way up the stairs and slapped my face so hard, I fell on the floor; quickly getting back up, I looked him in the eye as he slapped me again and walked down the stairs. He knew that I was out of his control and was no longer afraid of him.

It was a fad in school, that if you liked a boy, you wrote his name many times according to the amount of love you had. One day during one of Dad's unannounced room searches, he looked into my school folder and discovered that I had written a boys's name one thousand times. He became furious knowing that it was the black boy who lived next door. A decent person, and a basketball star in our school; although he never gave me any indication that he liked me. We never even held hands.

Dad tried to convince me that I no longer needed to attend school. He hoped that I would become like my siblings who dropped out of school at a young age. This would avoid me socializing with other children and become a full time housekeeper.

A short time later, our uncle Dillion arrived in his station wagon to get eight of us children, leaving James and Peter behind. I had no idea what was going on, and did not want to go, and I put on a performance in the front yard while the boys dragged me to the car. Aunt Flora never said a kind word during her few visits and I did not like her.

After arriving at her house, we immediately went from "rags to riches" with her mocking our raggedy clothes, held together with safety pins, as she took them off our bodies. After bathing us, she provided us with very expensive clothing she had stored from raising her four children. She said to me, "That dress costs fifty dollars."

We were told that our stay was for a short time, until another house could be provided for us. We were kept busy at all times, cleaning her three-story, expensively furnished home and scrubbing clothes in the wash tub, as we had to change our attire three times a day. She also cared for her three young grandchildren, whom her daughter had abandoned. They too became a part of our responsibility, and as usual, I carried the heavier load. Our only time out was when she was forced to leave the house for a few hours on business, taking Kelly with her, or when her clients arrived to have their fortunes told. We were either shoved upstairs and instructed not to make a sound or we were allowed to sit quietly in the yard. Although she lived on a street occupied by doctors and lawyers, no one knew we existed. There was no music and only once we watched a very small television, during one of Frank's rare visits, because he turned it on. Michael Jackson was a very little boy, and Frank said, "One day that little boy will be a big star."

During our stay there, our uncle came by a couple of times to see how things were. While our aunt Flora was chastising us, he made funny faces behind her back, sticking his tongue out at her and pulling on his ears. One day, he took us to the Brooklyn projects to visit his daughter, who never came around to see her own children. Auntie did not join us, as she would not be caught dead entering the projects to visit anyone; which explains why I never met her until recently. We arrived back at two in the morning, and were immediately sat at the table to eat our dinner.

She made such a fuss about our improper table manners, uncle said to her, "Please let the children eat. It is two o'clock in the morning. This is no time to teach them table manners!" He did not like the way she treated us, being a very kind person.

Although she did her best to provide for us, her nasty remarks about Mom being a low-class thief, stealing sheets and towels, and how we should be happy to be amongst rich people, eating and dressing like they do, were hard to hear. I resented that, along with her constant threats about reporting us to Dad if we did not obey her, and how we would get a beating. I had enough! Even though she provided me with cigarettes, I started talking back to her and if she attempted to assault me, I ran up to the third floor. She did not have the strength to make it up there. Later on I came down, knowing that she did not stay angry long.

She would inform us when our parents were going to arrive for their monthly visit, and then I was on my best behavior, even though her threats continued. Dad questioned Auntie about every move we made. I could see the hatred in his eyes when he looked at me, although she never reported my bad behavior. Once, during their visit, when Dad was conversing with her, I gave her a signal to sneak me a cigarette. She said to him, "Did you know that Nancy smokes cigarettes?" He made a gesture to hit me, but she authoritatively told him not to touch me, saying, "Here child, go and smoke." I took the two cigarettes and quickly ran upstairs to get out of his sight.

Linda, my seven-year-old second cousin, was infatuated with me, becoming a thorn in my side. Everything I did from morning to night revolved around her. I despised that, but there was nothing I could do about it.

After a few months, my parents arrived to take their children home, leaving me to stay with Auntie. I was not permitted to ever visit them, or even know where they lived.

Frank, a tall, thin handsome man at the dining room table, rolling a joint, while Auntie was upstairs in her bedroom. He probably wondered why I was left behind. In the fourteen years of my life, I had never held a conversation with any of my cousins. Jokingly, I said, "I like your cool cigarette. Can I smoke some?" In a deep New York accent, he said, "No." I smiled. Licking the paper, he said, "You're going to be a whore, just like your sister Susan." I knew why he said that; she gave him a french kiss during their good-byes, which no one knew I saw. I began singing a mocking song, and stuck my rear end out at him. He jumped up, broke a bottle, and started chasing me with it. I ran up the narrow staircase, screaming "Auntie Flora! Auntie Flora!" I ran into her room and hid behind her. After hearing all the commotion, my older cousin Gene, who I did not know lived in the house with his Jewish girlfriend, stepped out from his room, wearing a beautiful silk robe, asking, "What the hell is going on here? She is just a kid!" When Frank tried to explain, he repeated, "She is just a kid!"

Summer vacation was over, and my two second cousins, Michael, in kindergarden and Linda, in the second grade, went back to the Catholic school a few houses away. I was not enrolled in school. A perfect plan to keep me away from civilization. A prisoner in a big beautiful home in Floral Park, Long Island, where no one in the neighborhood knew that I existed.

One day, overhearing Uncle say to Flora that he was going to visit Dad, quietly I hid in the back of his car, lying flat on the floor. After about twenty-five minutes in transit, I popped my head up and said, "Hi, Uncle." Startled, he said, "Your auntie is going to kill me! She will have a fit when she discovers you are gone." He did not turn back.

It was apparent that each time we moved, our living conditions and neighborhood became more poverty-stricken. This time our family moved into a big green run down, tacky looking house in Central Islip. Whatever the conditions were, however, I did not want to go back to Auntie's house.

I related to Ma the things Auntie said about her stealing towels and other household items, and saying that she had never taught us table manners, and how we should feel privileged to be around people with class, enjoying rich people's food, mentioning that the pastry she brought for us children during her occasional visits was not given to us, but rather placed in her grandchildren's lunch boxes. Capturing her outrage, I then begged her not to send me back there.

There was a fight, Dad trying to hit me with his fists, while I hid behind Ma, avoiding his blows. She told him that I was not going back there and repeated the things his sister said about her. He stopped when she started swinging at him, causing Uncle to separate them. Giving in, he said to me, "If you stay here, you will have to walk a straight line." I wore the same clothing for a few months; no longer the housemaid but rather an intruder that he did not want around. Held with an iron fist, he made it impossible for me to remain there.

I was enrolled in Central Islip High School and had to walk through the woods to the school bus stop. There were a lot of black children in line, and only one red-haired, freckle-faced white girl named Kathy at the end. The girls told her that she better not get on the bus, or they would kick her ass. My first time being there, I responded, "You will have to kick my ass first, before you kick her ass!" Since there were five buses, we waited for the last bus, and became friends; she was also new in town. Praise God, I had no idea that she was my ticket out of Dad's house. Kathy's mother was thrilled about her daughter having a friend, and welcomed me into her home. She was very industrious and made all of Kathy's clothes. I arrived at her house in the morning, washed, and changed into her beautiful clothes. After breakfast we brushed our teeth, put on makeup, and went to school. After school, we went to her home and I changed back into my clothes, wiped my makeup off, and returned home. Kathy periodically hitch-hiked to Long Beach to see her Puerto Rican boyfriend named Jaime and also visiting her grandmother and would stay there for a couple of weeks. We always talked about how someday she would take me there.

When I saw Dad spending many hours in the bathroom, I knew he was going away for a number of days. I too prepared myself to leave for the weekend, with big pink rollers in my hair and wearing Mom's robe so it wouldn't be noticed that I was dressed up. I had a very decent Puerto Rican boyfriend named David, who had the utmost respect for me, never touching me in a wrong manner. He was my first boyfriend whom I met through Kathy and Jaime. David lived in Long Beach, Long Island. When Dad left, I took the rollers out and got ready to go. After a couple of times, Peter asked to join me, and he too made friends out there. We children alway hitch-hiked on the Southern State Parkway. Ma never mentioned a word about us leaving.

One day Kelly asked if she could go along with me. When we arrived home, the children quickly notified me that I was going to be beaten. Dad attacked me in the kitchen, punching me with his fists. When I hit the floor, he began kicking me, while Mom along with the weekend visitors watched, questioning why Kelly was not chastised or given a beaten.

One day while Mom was in the bathroom putting on makeup, getting ready for work, I told her that I was going to kill him. "I'll wait until he is asleep, and I am going to stab him with a knife." He was in the next room pretending to be asleep. He jumped up, grabbed a knife and put it in my hand saying, "Go ahead and kill me!" When she was leaving for work, I said, "Ma, I've got to go. When you come home, I will not be here." She said, "Where will you go?" I said, "In the streets." She said, "Okay." I went to Kathy's house to leave with her for Long Beach, but missed her by a few minutes. Her nine-year-old brother Jacky said, "Nancy, I know how to get to Long Beach. I'll take you there." I took a little brown bag with a pair of shorts and a blouse in it and we left. When we arrived in Long Beach, I received warm greetings from Kathy and all her friends, who became my friends too.

Although Kathy's mother Laura was a jewel, she could have cared less about what her daughter did. To avoid school, Kathy did not go back home. She and I stayed at different friends' homes, boosting our clothing and panhandling for food. Periodically, we visited her mother for the weekend.

Dad must have been informed about me being in the neighborhood, because he drove around and saw Peter, Kathy, and I walking down the street. He got out of his car to pursue me. We climbed a barbed wire fence and when I reached the top to jump over, my fishnet stockings got caught in the wire and I could not break them loose. He was fast approaching when Peter ran back to the rescue, moments before Dad could have grabbed me. We ran away laughing.

Jaime's aunt Juanita, needed someone to babysit her two children while she and her husband were at work. They lived in a one-bedroom apartment in Long Beach, above the bay. My services paid for my room and board although Juanita bought me new clothes, boots, and other necessities. I really enjoyed staying there, and she even welcomed Peter and Jacky when they came to visit, giving them a seat at the dinner table.

Even though Juanita had love for me, after three months she kindly asked to leave, but without a real explanation. Her husband Carlos was about fifteen years younger than she was, and possibly she felt insecure about us living in such close quarters. Whatever her reason was, I was back on the street, teaming up with another runaway girl named Nora, who I'd previously met through Kathy. She too was in love with my boyfriend, and we became friends. The lady she was living with Rita agreed to take me in, too. Rita weighed about three hundred and fifty pounds, with a husband that looked like a giant. Our job was to take care of their four children and quietly clean their dirty house, without waking her husband, who slept during the day.

Drinking hard liquor, popping pills, and dating men was this Rita's game. When her men friends arrived, we were told to remain in the basement until she left with them. Then we were permitted to come up and drink the balance of the booze and pop whatever pills she left for us.

Now it was time to do the housework. In the basement was a six-foot-high pile of dirty clothes. I said to Nora, "How are we going to clean all these clothes?" We started with the kitchen. Having never seen a dishwasher before, I stacked the dirty dishes in there, added a cup of laundry detergent, and pushed the "on" button. Then we went to the basement to do clothes. When were returned to the kitchen, it was filled with suds. More suds than I have ever seen in my life! We quickly cleaned it up before Rita came back home.

Peter occasionally arrived on the weekends to party and to see how I was coming along. During this time in my life, he was kinder to me than anyone else in the family. One weekend he said that Mom was upset, learning that I was out on the streets and that she would appreciate it if I would consider staying with Susan and her husband Jose, who was willing to provide for me and send me to school. I agreed just to get away from that miserable place.

When I arrived at their home in Newark, New Jersey, I was enrolled in Barringer High School. I was an outcast in the neighborhood because New York style clothing had not yet reached New Jersey. My wardrobe consisted of mini-skirts, skin tight pants with big bell bottoms, skin-tight boots, and a leather jacket with a STP sticker on the back.

After attending school for a couple of months, Jose left work early to pick me up from school. Noticing a boy grabbing me in a head lock, he jumped out of his car and punched the guy, telling him that he better not ever put his hands on me again. When I got into the car, after a couple of minutes he asked me, "Did Vicki's husband ever have sex with you? I know that he had sex with Sally." I said, "No, he did not." He further inquired, "He never tried anything with you?" I answered, "No, he never tried anything with me." Of course I lied. I was only a little girl when that happened. Now I was a high-school student. Jose left his job early to spend time alone with me, to talk about sex. When we arrived at the tiny one-and-a-half bedroom apartment that had no doors to separate the rooms other than the bathroom, Susan asked Jose, "Why are you home early?" He answered, "I left work early to pick Nancy up from school." That raised a red flag and she went ballistic. That was only the beginning. He was on a mission that revolved around me and would last for years.

Peter came to visit me, wearing skin-tight pants with skin-tight boots. The teenagers that hung out on the corner called me a whore and him a faggot.

One evening while Peter and I were walking down the street towards Susan's apartment, a boy named Frank, a good-looking Puerto Rican guy, crossed the street from the corner where he hung out with the other teenagers, and asked for our hand in friendship. Shortly after that, he became my boyfriend.

I was subjected to cleaning dishes, scrubbing floors, washing laundry, and cooking dinner after school, while Susan lounged on the couch eating potato chips and drinking soda, watching television. When Jose came home, she jumped off the couch to show him that the housework had been done—and the cooking that *she* did, all the time winking her eye at me. After I had attended high school for about four months as an A student, they informed me that I had to quit school and seek employment to pay them room and board.

Susan and I got a job in Belleville, working in a factory earning forty-two dollars a week. Kelly and their friend soon joined us.

At night when the family went to sleep, I cried over having to quit school. Children my age were on their way to school with their friends, carrying books, while I was at the bus stop, on my way to work an eight-hour shift in a factory and having to lie about my age because I was only fourteen. Even worse, after work, my household duties were waiting for me.

When Susan got married, she weighed about a hundred and ten pounds with long, beautiful black hair that reached below her waist. Two years later, she weighed three hundred and sixty pounds and was cutting her hair just below her ears.

This was the first time Susan had a little freedom, and undertaking a crash diet, she lost more than two hundred pounds. She was going to exercise that right by dating a tall handsome Italian man named Carmen who worked at the diner we frequented for lunch who was unlike the gorilla looking Puerto Rican man she married.

Frank and I were her ticket out of the apartment at night, for walks to the Branch Brook Park, where she met with Carmen to have sex in the bushes on numerous occasions—until he got busted having sex with the old lady who worked with him at the diner. Susan became indignant when she learned that his wife caught them in action. Not being able to live it down, she quit her job after four months of work.

One night while sitting in front of our two-story, two-apartment building on Broadway, enjoying the evening with our neighbor, a car filled with Italian guys from the factory where we worked arrived to call on Susan. They'd heard about her affair. They had been drinking and were wild. One guy started screaming for Susan. "Susan, come here. I want to talk to you!" She said, "I don't know who you are." Sarcastically, he said, "I'm Danny boy, Susan. Now you know who I am, come over here, so Danny boy can talk to you." When she did not respond, he got louder. "Susan, Danny boy wants to talk to you!" Our neighbor's husband came out with a broom, chasing after the car as they drove away. Alarmed, Susan picked up her folding chair and went inside. She remained scared for a few days and hoped they would not return to expose her.

After paying for my room and board, the majority of the money went to Mom. I also bought her fine china, and clothes for the children. After a while, though, Jose said that I was not allowed to have money. My paychecks were to be signed over to him until the end of my stay, and whatever was left over after my expenses would be returned to me.

He made it very hard for me to spend time with Frank, taxing me with more chores. His jealousy became overwhelming, and he tormented me constantly, making nasty remarks about Frank, indicating that he was gay, and much more. He took my ring that Frank had given me from the bathroom sink, and after many days of enjoying my suffering, he returned it to me, making sure that I knew he had the power to make me suffer. Another Daddy situation, but in a different form.

Life started to get harder as he made up more reasons why I could not go out after work. One afternoon, Frank came to call on me for a date. After my chores were completed, I asked permission to leave. They agreed. When I returned about five hours later, Jose answered the door with a look of terror on his face. He asked me to quickly get my things and leave and said that Susan was in the hospital getting her stomach pumped out because she had tried to commit suicide and that it would be best if she did not see me when she returned. I grabbed my clothes and took a bus to Vicki's house in Linden, New Jersey.

I lived with Vicki for a couple of weeks, becoming her household maid. When Frank came to visit me, she dressed in my clothes, with the intention of enticing him. Because she was twice my size, I kindly asked her to please stop wearing my clothes, and walked away. She grabbed an iron pipe and struck me on the head with it, causing a concussion. I went to James and his wife next door and lay on the couch in their living room. James telephoned Mom and Dad to tell them what had happened. They immediately notified Kelly, who arrived two and a half hours later from Long Island, terrified at my condition. Susan and Jose arrived before her to verify my condition, with Susan weeping, saying that if it was not for her, this would not have happened.

I did not speak to Vicki for three years after that. Kelly took me to a house on Long Island where she rented a room on the second floor from a lady who lived there. I remained in bed for two weeks while she nursed me back to health. She worked at the Pilgrim State Hospital. She bought me clothes, combed my hair, did my makeup, and tried her best to do whatever she could to make me feel better. I never saw a doctor, and I suffered for years with headaches. Kelly was a nightclub person, dragging me all over New York City and Long Island chasing after bands.

About a month later, Susan and Jose pleaded with me to return to them, and I did, for Frank's sake. Months later, Jose had enough money to buy a home. Noticing that Frank and I were very much in love, and that I not only had a "going steady" ring but was wearing an engagement ring, he conjured up a new scheme by moving far away from Newark to a town called Laurence Harbor, where we knew no one, and forcing me see Frank only on the week-end. His insane jealously of this schoolboy encouraged him to brainwash Susan to develop a deep hatred towards Frank also, making it almost impossible for us to see each other. When Susan went into the hospital to have her third child, I took the opportunity to move out. I was not going to be a live-in Nanny caring for her child during the night.

On the other hand, Frank was abused by his alcoholic father, who hated me with a deep passion. Frank and I saw each other in secret, and his father alerted the neighbors to notify him if we were seen together; if so, Frank received a beating. He eventually was forced to move out of his father's house and went to live in East Orange with his brother and family.

I asked Frank to find us a room to rent before Susan's baby was born, and he did. Jose gave me the balance of the money he was holding for me—four hundred and fifty dollars—while he detailed my expenses. When he left to the hospital to visit Susan, who was to come home the following day, I quickly packed my belongings and left with Frank, who was waiting down the street. When Jose got back home, to his surprise, I was gone.

We lived in Newark in a tiny room, only big enough for a single size bed, in a boarding house. We had nothing but a bed and an alarm clock. Although that room did not provide us heat in the winter, we kept our milk outside on the roof when it snowed. The owner was an old lady named Katherine who adored us because we were there only to sleep and most weekends we were in Long Island, at my parents' home. Six months later, we moved to a larger room in the same house, one that had a full size bed with a refrigerator.

My first order of business was to immediately sign myself back into school. I was now seventeen and had been absent for three years. The principal at Barringer High School said that I needed my parents to enroll me. I told him that I lived with my grandmother, using her address as my place of residence, the Seventh Street Projects, which were only a few blocks away. I knew this was the most dangerous place to be if you were a white man dressed in a suit. He said that she needed to come in to enroll me. I explained to him that she was bed-ridden and that he needed to go there for her to sign the papers. He then said to the clerk, "Enroll her into school."

Had he entered those projects, he might not have made it out in one piece. They put human waste all over the elevator buttons and piss in the elevator, forcing you to walk up the stairs in total darkness, because all the light bulbs had been removed by the thugs who were waiting for you.

Months later, I told Katherine that I could not make it to the school dance, because I did not have a dress. She said, "Oh, yes, you are going to that dance." She took me around the corner to a fancy little dress shop and told the lady that I was her daughter. Although I was pregnant, she made sure that I had a very pretty dress.

Frank and I went to school from eight o'clock in the morning until three-thirty in the afternoon; and then we went to work from four-thirty to twelve midnight.

Because I was pregnant, we wanted to get married, but Frank's parents refused to sign the papers; we both were underage and needed their permission. Mom asked them three times to please sign the papers. During my fifth month of pregnancy I took the liberty of visiting Frank's parents, to ask them to sign the papers. His father grabbed me by the throat and tried to push me down the staircase; I held onto the railing for dear life. I weighed only one hundred pounds. I could not hold on any longer and just as I was about to let go, he stopped. Frank's mother stood by and watched.

Frank started falling behind in his grades, and my history teacher informed me that his history teacher told her that he was in danger of not graduating if he did not get at least a B grade on his term paper.

He was aware that I would not marry him if he flunked out of school. We stayed awake almost three days, cramming him for his term paper he wrote (and had to memorize) on automation. He received a high score and graduated.

CHAPTER NINE

The Wedding Reception and Married Life at Dad's

After graduation, Frank and I moved into my parents' home because the baby was coming in a couple of months and I was still a minor and still their responsibility; and the fact was, I knew nothing about having a baby. Mom had real concerns about getting me married before the baby was born. Back then, if you had a baby and you were not married, the baby took the grandfather's name. Ma did not need any more dependents. She made a trip to Frank's parents' and his mother finally agreed to sign the papers, under the condition that Frank remained in their home for two weeks prior to the wedding, During that time they invited family members and other girls to a beach party, trying to convince him that he was too young to understand what love was and that all he needed to do was support the baby. When their attempts failed, they said, "Have it your way."

It became very difficult preparing for the wedding, needing a ride to Newark for blood tests and the marriage license, with Jonathan as our only source of transportation. He agreed to take us, at our expense, because he too had business to take care of in Linden, New Jersey, trying to legally get his child back from Vicki.

Frank, Mom, Peter, and I piled into Jonathan's car. When Jonathan finished his business, it was dark, cold, and raining, with no time left to make it to city hall. Aggravated and frustrated, I tore the money for the marriage license into little pieces and threw it out the window. Jonathan threatened to hurt me. After an hour or so of listening to him, I jumped out of the car and hid from them in the bushes, getting drenched and watching them circle around the block many times before I made my presence known, then running down the street and forcing them to chase me. Mom instructed Frank and Peter to catch me for her, and they did, holding me down on the street until Mom approached, hitting me with her slipper and saying, "You son of a bitch. You better behave yourself!"

We finally were able to complete our business on the next trip to the city. Now we could get married. However, after all the calamities we had gone through, I had reached the point of doubting whether or not I wanted to get married. My mind changed about three times before I decided to go through with it.

Our wedding day arrived and Dad agreed to take us to the church. I thought for once that he was going to do something right, for a change. He adorned himself for four hours and then walked outside to warm the old junker up. Mother and I got our things together, and as we were approaching the car, he drove away, leaving us standing in the driveway.

Mother asked the old man who lived next door to please drive us to the train station, and he did, leaving us in a deserted place. We did not know when the train would arrive. I carried a cheap-looking suitcase containing a pink dress that cost sixteen dollars, a pair of borrowed gold colored shoes, and a homemade pink veil, made with material I bought for four dollars. That was my wedding apparel. About two hours later the Long Island train arrived and we boarded. After changing trains and buses, we reached our destination, a friend's house three houses away from Frank's parents' house, so that I could change into my wedding clothes.

Frank met us there dressed in a suit and shoes he had borrowed from his brother. Frank, Mom and I walked past his parents' house to catch the bus to the church. His parents were outside painting the front of their house and would not even look at us as we passed by.

Our wedding took place in the prayer chapel of a very big, beautiful old Presbyterian church on Broadway in downtown Newark; it was the only church that would marry us, because of my pregnancy. Mother and Manuel (Frank's brother) stood as witnesses. The ceremony went very quickly and soon we were on our way back to Brentwood, Long Island. We had planned a very small reception, a small cake and a few treats. That evening Dad came home and joined in the party, acting as though nothing had happened. He had the audacity to stand up and give a phony speech. Jonathan, James, and their wives were there, and everyone else except Susan, Vicki, and their families. They were not aware of the reception, nor were they invited. We received no gifts and did not expect any.

Prior to our marriage, while living at home, we were forced to treat each other as friends as opposed to lovers; Frank slept in the remodeled basement, and I upstairs in the girls' room. Mother and I had already arranged where Frank and I were going to sleep on our wedding night, and she let me borrow one of her nice nightgowns. The reception was over and it was time to go to bed. Dad insisted that our sleeping arrangements remain the same, but Mother made it clear that we were going to sleep together. "They are married now, for crying out loud!" she yelled.

What a bad dream that night turned out to be. It was unfortunate that we had four little girls sleeping in the same room with us, but Kelly acted as though it was her wedding night too, seducing Frank's brother Manuel many times over in different parts of the house and in the basement. At first he thought it was fun, but after a few hours, he began to get tired and sore. He tried to get away from her, but she would not let him go. He crept into our room with her holding his hand and whispered in Frank's ear to let him sleep with us in our single bed. I refused. Dad conveniently disappeared, so that she could have her fun.

The next morning, Ma and I were in the kitchen laughing quietly as I told her about last night's events between Manuel and Kelly, when suddenly she walked in, describing the large size of his penis. Ma wanted to hear more details as she loves that kind of talk. Kelly started talking about the blow job she gave him; I said that that was disgusting and wanted to exit the scene.

During my stay at home, I was under Dad's rule again, asking permission to go anywhere, with his looks giving me the answer. If I really needed to get away with my husband, I told him that I would be back in a few hours and not wait for a response. Sometimes he would look for me, knowing that I could only be at Kelly's bachelor apartment a few towns away.

I worked the night shift that ended at midnight in a yarn factory. Dad was my only transportation to and from work, and he decided one night not to pick me up. When work ended, everyone got into their cars and left, confident that I was also going to be picked up. After standing in front of the factory for thirty minutes, I realized that he was not going to arrive. It was very scary standing in that dark, deserted industrial area without a soul around or any sign of civilization.

A black man in his mid-fifties drove up in a Cadillac and asked me if he could be of some help. I told him I needed a ride home because my father must have had car trouble. This stranger said he would gladly take me home. After getting into the car and discovering that there were no handles to open the door, I began to panic in a cool way. He informed me that he was not going to take me home, but rather to Montauk Point, which is at the end of Long Island. Suffolk County during that time was country living, and the further you drive, the more deserted it becomes. He further stated that we were going to party and have a good time. Eight months pregnant with child was bad enough; now

I had a maniac or perhaps even a killer on my hands. Whether or not he was aware of my pregnancy, I do not know. Rest assure of one thing, I was in a bad situation, and I knew I had better use my survival tactics to save my life and my child.

Talking smooth was one of my specialties; I put my thinking cap on quickly. I'd already made the mistake of telling him that my husband would gladly take care of him when we get home. Forgetting that remark, I began to play his game, while driving down the parkway, pretending to feel comfortable, explaining how I loved to party, and after a hard night's work I desperately needed a party right about now; all the while moving closer to him, maybe touching his shoulder to show what an outgoing person I was.

Next, I took over, making the scheming look like my idea. I slipped in the idea that we must first go home to inform Mother that I was okay so that she would not stay up all night worrying about me, or perhaps getting the police involved. He said, "I can't let you go home, because your husband won't let you back out." I said, in a forceful and believable tone, "Oh, yes, he will! I am going to introduce you as my foreman, telling him that you have an overabundance of work that needs to be done, and that you are going to pay me time and a half for doing so." He fell for it and backtracked to my home.

We arrived home about one a.m. and sure enough, the whole family, including the in-laws, were waiting for me. When the car pulled into the driveway, everyone rushed out of the house to greet me. I got out of the car and introduced the stranger to Mom and Frank as my foreman. Everyone else gathered around the car to look at the black beast, who was so ugly, one could hardly look at him. Frank shook his hand, and Mother gave him blessings while thanking him. I walked into the house with no intention of ever seeing him again. The crowd stayed outside with him for about five minutes until one of the girls ran inside to tell me that he was waiting for me. I said to her, "Tell him to leave without me."

My sister-in-law followed me into the house, and I told her the story of what had taken place, unaware that Dad was sitting quietly nearby, not making his presence known until about the end of my story. He then made a gruesome remark: "The man should have killed you." That was the last time I ever worked on Long Island.

Summer vacation was over, and I enrolled at Brentwood High School. A month prior to the baby's arrival, the board of education provided tutors to school me at home. Dad liked that idea, broadcasting to the neighbors how he provided tutors for his daughter to be educated at home. I kept to myself most of the time, keeping the house in order and studying. When family members arrived to visit, I took my books out and stayed occupied with my studies while continuing to be alert about what was going on around me.

Jonathan and his wife came by often, each seemingly closer to death—their thin bodies, the dark rings around their eyes from the use of the hypodermic needle; the fake tones in their voices, trying to hide their broken spirits since they'd lost their child.

One evening during their visit, I was inspired to talk with them. They were very attentive, and happy that I even acknowledged them. I asked them if they were still interested in getting their child back, and of course they said yes. Being close to the time of having my baby, I normally would not have gone far from the house; but this time I was willing to go any distance to execute the kidnapping that I spontaneously planned. My short stay with Vicki and her family in Linden, Jersey, three years earlier, had allowed me to memorize their daily routine. I knew exactly how to escape with the child. Vicki and her husband left for work at six a.m., meaning that we had to leave Long Island at four o'clock to get there in time for the kidnapping. Frank, Jonathan, Sherri, Kelly and I were the only ones who knew about the plan. Kelly certainly was not going to squeal; she was their drug partner.

That evening we all slept at Kelly's apartment to ensure no mistakes. We were on schedule as planned. We parked down the street and watched Vicki and her husband drive away to work. Jonathan and I went to their apartment and I knocked on the door and Sally, who was babysitting, asked, "Who is it?" I said, "Nancy." She opened the door, and when she saw Jonathan, she said, "Oh, no!" He walked into the apartment, picked up the child, and we were on our way back to Long Island. The couple was so happy. Jonathan took Frank and I back to the house and we acted like nothing had happened. Mother could alway sense when something was going on. She gave me a look as if to say, "Well, are you going to tell me what happened?" I pretended not to notice her glance and walked past her. She would eventually find out.

Two days later, Jonathan and his wife arrived with the look of death on their faces. Speaking in a low voice, he said, "Vicki kidnapped the child back." I said, "You are kidding me. Don't joke about things like that." Then I saw the tears roll down his cheeks, and realized that he was not kidding. He and his wife went to work at the Pilgrim State Hospital while the baby's grandmother babysat, leaving him unattended for a moment on the front lawn. They snatched him up and drove away. Vicki abused all her children with severe beatings and verbal abuse.

Shortly after this incident, Jonathan encouraged Sally to report to the school principal (she and I were registered at that time but I was no longer attending school) about the forced incest between her and Dad.

The children went off to school, Frank went to work, leaving Mother, Dad and myself in the house. It seemed quiet and desolate; I wondered why Mom did not go to work that day. She and Dad stayed in their bedroom. I sat in the dinning room preparing for my next day's school work, when suddenly they both appeared, Dad asking Mom, "Should we tell her?" I said, "Tell me what?" Dad immediately walked away, leaving Mother to tell me the story. She told me about the incident that had taken place at the school. That explained why she was not at work; having an appointment to see the school principal. Mother's face appeared as though death was written on it, and Dad was more frightened than I have ever seen him before. They kept this secret until the very last minute before revealing it to me.

Suddenly, I felt very sorry for Mom and Dad. For once in their lives, they were totally dependent upon my help to get them out of this mess. Maybe I should not have helped them, but I did. The abuse I experienced as a child and teenager, did not change the love that I had for my parents. I loved my mother very much. I didn't realize the extent of the abuse, until I described and re-lived it in this book.

Those cowards, Jonathan and Sally and possibly Peter could have thought of a way more challenging way to get even with Dad, long before this time. There was thirteen of us, and only one of him. We should have been able to overtake him.

I said to Mom, "I will go with you to the school and tell the Principal that the accusation against Dad is not true." She immediately went into the her room to tell Dad. I got dressed in minutes, and we were on our way to the school. That was the quickest Dad was ever ready to take us anywhere. He dropped us off a block away from the school, and drove away fast.

The attendance office directed us to the principal's office. The principal spoke to Mother as though she had already been tried and convicted. He was very sure of himself, having the intention of taking the other children away and Dad thrown in jail, destroying the "demonic dynasty." I abruptly interrupted the principal, demanding that he watch how he spoke to my mother. He then asked who I was and I gave him my name and credentials. I said, "I am an 'A' student and my father's daughter. He never expressed any of this intolerant behavior around me." After checking Sally's failing grades against my achievements, he deeply apologized and shook our hands goodbye. Little did he know my parents took no credit for my academic achievements. Do not forget, I was still with child and needed to have a baby and live at home with my parents.

It was a surprise to see that Dad did not make us wait hours to be picked up. He was quite prompt, waiting for us on the side street. After hearing the good news, he was happy for the moment; and this incident never was mentioned again.

When we first moved in with my parents, Frank did not get a job, but rather hung out with James and Peter, who taught him bad manners. Sometimes I did not see him for a few days. James told Frank, "Kick her ass if she doesn't like it." Frank was enjoying a little freedom, something he did not have at his parents' home or after he left home and was going to school during the day and working at night. But when he did get a job working at a factory, he fell in love with another girl.

Once at two o'clock in the morning Sally entered our bedroom in the remodeled basement to inform Frank that his girlfriend was down the street waiting for him. I fought with him not to go but he left anyway. When he came back a short time later, because I was so angry, he locked himself in the bathroom and turned the light out. I then took a piece of newspaper and stuck it under the door and lit a match to it. All he saw in that little dark bathroom was large flames coming from the only exit. When he got out he assaulted me, but I did not mention it to anyone. I went into labor and the following night was rushed to the hospital. Dad, Mom, and Frank and I got into that small Datsun and were on our way through the cold, dark, rainy November night. Although Smithtown was not far away from Brentwood, it seemed like it took forever to get there.

After we arrived, Frank went to the men's room to groom his hair; during his absence, the nurse came with a wheelchair and wheeled me into the elevator and then to the pre-delivery room where I changed into hospital attire and was placed in a crib. They gave me a shot of some kind of drug and tied me down. The room began to spin and I felt like I was on a trip, remembering that Kelly told me that this same doctor stole one of her twins that he delivered.

In the next room, doctors and nurses were playing cards, laughing, and having a good time. They would not even answer my calls. After a couple of hours a nurse finally came to ask me what I wanted. I said to her, "Please let me go home. I'll forget the whole thing and you can forget about it too." She then punched me in my stomach twice, saying that it would help induce labor. After twenty-four hours, they gave me a shot that put me to sleep. When I awoke, the baby had been born.

During my three-day stay at the hospital, I received no phone call, flowers, cards, or visitors. The evening before I was released, Mother, Dad, and Frank arrived two minutes before visiting hours were over. In my anger, I said, "Get out of my room. I do not want to see your faces!" Dad and Frank left, but Mom became furious at the way I had spoken to Dad, forcing me into the restroom and hitting me with her slipper. I tried to call for the nurse, but Mom became even angrier saying, "How dare you call for the nurse! You want the nurse, you son of a bitch. I'll give you the nurse," while continuing to hit me. Then she left the room.

The following morning, while packing my belongings, fear began to creep in. I began to wonder if Dad was going to pick me up, or would he pull one of his stunts by not showing? If he did not arrive by eleven, I would have to remain another day in the hospital, as was their policy.

Dad arrived to the hospital to pick me up and we went home. He prepared the bed in his room for the baby and me to rest in. The girls stayed home from school that day because of the excitement of a new baby, arguing over whose turn it was to hold the baby.

A rich businessman who lived down the street, Mr. Ludlow, gave me beautiful baby furniture, clothes, and everything that a baby needed, from their last baby.

Soon William, our infant had pneumonia and Mother and Kelly assured me that they knew how to nurse him back to health. It was amazing the amount of care and time Kelly put into nursing him. She kept watch over him all night, continuously sucking mucus from his nose so that he could breath, and he recovered.

After his recovery, Mom and Dad were eager to get rid of us, even though Frank was paying her rent for our stay. Dad wanted money, too, but Mom took it and told us not to let him know.

One day I arrived home from school and saw Dad placing a lock on the basement door, effectively confiscating everything we owned. He was a very sick man, possessed of a legion of demons, who controlled his actions; plus, he needed his "incest quarters" back. I was cramping his style.

Through some miracle, a friend arrived to visit me that day that I had brought to Long Island with us when we left Newark. I had not seen him in three months, and forgot that he existed. I packed a few of my sister's clothes, took the diaper bag, and said good-bye to Ma. Frank had not been around for three days. I said to my gay friend, "Let's go back to Newark," and we left, hitch-hiking down the Southern State Parkway and over the Verrazano Bridge. We arrived in Long Island together and I hadn't seen him until now, and now we were going back together.

I was glad my time was up at home. My baby had gotten sick from lack of heat, my husband was hanging around with my brothers, and he was cheating on me.

When we arrived in Newark, we kissed goodbye, and never saw each other again. I went to the Seventh Avenue Projects, to Grandma's, and told her that Dad had kicked me out and I needed a place to stay until I could get situated. She welcomed the baby and me. Shortly afterwards, Frank arrived and we moved into an apartment.

CHAPTER TEN

Frank and I on Own Own Again

Frank and I moved to South Broad Street in Newark, into a furnished apartment building occupied predominantly by black homosexuals. There were about eight rooms that all shared one bathroom. Every kind of disease imaginable was floating around that place. Our room consisted of a single bed, one broken dresser, a roach-infested stove, and a small refrigerator. The rats were as big as cats and roaches were as big as water bugs.

I was somewhat naive about babies, so a gay guy named Liz tried to counsel me concerning the baby's cleanliness; stating that I must make sure that the milk was thoroughly washed from the baby's fingers and mouth to ensure that the rats would not chew the baby' s fingers off. The baby slept in the top drawer, the only drawer that was not broken, wrapped in my clothing as a blanket. In below-zero weather, the manager tuned the heat off at eight o'clock in the evening and did not turn it back on until nine o'clock in the morning, making things difficult for us and for the baby, who shortly afterwards caught pneumonia. The freezing weather came through the poorly insulated windows that were covered with dingy plastic curtains may have also contributed to the pneumonia; as I needed a few changes of clothes from my little sisters to wear to school.

Anxious to continue my education, I went back to the same school I attended prior to our son's birth. This time the high school principal made it hard for me to register in the school, which had racial problems. The staff was all white, and I was placed in the Hispanic category. Each day, for five days in a row, from eight o'clock in the morning until the end of the school day, I sat waiting to be registered, being told at the end of each day that there was not enough time to register me.

The following Monday, I went to the board of education in Newark and reported the matter to the director, Dr. Einstein. I explained to him that I was a A student and that I had sat in the Barringer High School office for five days without being registered. Practically in tears, I said that the principal was asking me personal questions, such as about my marriage, knowing that I had a baby. There are billboards all over town saying "Get A High School Education" and yet I could not get registered. The director calmly sat me down in the lobby, and went into his office. He telephoned the school and after about five minutes or so, returned and shook my hand, saying that I should return to school immediately to be registered. I deeply thanked him for his help, and he said no problem, that he was glad to do one more good deed before retiring, as that was his last day.

When I got to the school, the principal called me into his office and asked me, "I did not ask you that personal question, did I ?" I told him in a deliberate manner, "Yes, you did ask me that."

He immediately and very politely sent me to get registered. The same ladies who enjoyed watching me sit there all week, suddenly became very attentive and overly kind towards me. While speaking to my counselor about what subjects I wanted to take, one of the office attendants, who obviously was not informed, walked in and asked what I was doing there. My counselor whispered to her that special orders were to not ask any questions. The woman then walked out.

My counselor assigned my schedule, exchanging my college prep courses for study halls, homemaking, art, and other minor courses that usually were presented to the blacks and Latinos. I demanded to be enrolled in the courses that I wanted and was qualified for, requesting that my lunch period be exchanged for a major course. She said that it was against the law to give me all of those classes without a lunch break, but she did it anyway.

Still sore at Frank for his involvement with the other woman, I became numb towards anything other than getting an education and taking care of the baby the best way I knew how. My behavior was out of control, forcing me out of love with him, even though he was still a teenager, fresh out of high school. My family liked him very much, especially Mom, because he did whatever she asked him to do. Dad enjoyed the fact that he was so naive, using him for whatever he wanted him for, such as having him work on some temporary job he managed to get and leaving Frank there all day to work, without food or water. My brothers loved him too, because of his innocence; they had him take a turn on stealing the goods before the stores opened and pushing Dad's car down the street, so the engine could not be heard, after they stole the keys.

When Frank came home from work, I left with Sally, (who also moved into the building) and sometimes Liz, to the gay bar. Sometimes he tried to bring me home, and when I refused, he dragged me out of the bar and into the streets coaxing me to leave with him. I was outraged at the conditions we were forced to live in. Sally did not mind because she was a hype heroin addict.

The winter was over and one day Frank came home from work and said, "I have something to show you." Frank's brother drove us to the better side of town where we entered a house on Mount Pleasant Avenue, two blocks up the hill from the Passaic River that had a newly remodeled "doll house" type of an apartment that consisted of one bedroom, one bathroom, and a nice little kitchen, on the third floor. It was owned by a little old lady named Parrot, who kept things in excellent order. This woman had sharp eyes, and observed every move anyone made; not hesitating to inform you how loud your urine was during the middle of the night. We made fun of her but nonetheless, I was happy and felt safe living there. I was willing to forgive Frank for breaking my heart, and my life instantly changed. I was never going back to South Broad Street again. I even acquired a wonderful fifteen-year-old babysitter who lived on the first floor with a much older man. One day they moved away quickly, without an announcement and I was once again in need of a babysitter. Living in the worst ghetto in America, we did not have Day Care Centers, nor did they exist at that time. Factory workers and store employees did not earn enough money to pay for that expense. Working class people or school children such as myself, depended on neighborhood women or family members who stayed at home to care for their children, while they went to work or school.

I arrived one weekend with William who was already walking, talking, and potty trained and told Ma that I no longer had a babysitter and that I needed someone to care for my child while I went to school. She said, "I'll have to ask your father." When she came back, she said, "Your father said that it is okay." Of course, we needed his permission, as he was the only one left in the house after everyone went to school, and Mom went to work. I departed from my son feeling great remorse and missing him so much. I telephoned Mother at work every day, asking how he was doing. Finally she got tired of it and said, "He is doing the same as he was the day before." When we visited the following weekend, Ma told Frank, "Tell your wife to stop calling me on my job, asking how the baby is doing." About two and a half months later, I found another great babysitter.

I became pregnant with my second child, and Dad made such a mockery of that until the the board of education reviewed the eleventh graders' SATs (Scholastic Aptitude Test), choosing the twenty top students with the highest scores from all the high schools in Newark to participate in an IBM keypunch course to learn how to operate wall-sized computers during summer vacation. I was one of the twenty. We hitch-hiked to Long Island to show my parents the letter which had to be signed and returned to the board.

I was able to hide my pregnancy under my long black cape that had a hood. During the winter season, almost every girl wore one. When summer arrived, I continued to wear my cape.

One hot afternoon while walking down the quiet corridor, I heard the principal complaining to a teacher about how distressed he was to slip on a banana peel while walking down the hallway or to find a half-eaten sandwich in the drinking fountain. When he looked up and saw me walking in their direction, bewilderment came over him; he was always hesitant to speak to me after the incident concerning my registration. He approached me in a polite manner and said, "Can I ask you a question?" I said yes. He said, "Let's go into this classroom"—which was empty. We three entered the room, and after we sat down, he asked me why I was wearing that big heavy coat when it was a hundred degrees outside. I began to laugh so hard that he stood up in disgust and left the room. I had no intention of telling him that I was pregnant again. He would have forced me to attend night school, which they tried towards the end of my pregnancy.

Sally hooked up with an elderly black man named Lou who was a bank robber and also held up liquor stores. They too moved into Parrot's house. She had a table stacked with money and never gave me a dime. She left for the weekend, leaving her door open with a table full of money, but I did not touch one cent. One time I cleaned her apartment for seventy-five dollars.

Sally had an obsession with gay guys, dressing in drag, posing as a homosexual, which having a flat chest made believable. She went to New York City to pass out money to the gay junkies after each robbery, taking me along for the ride. Once I asked Sally to please let me clean her apartment so that I could pay for my high-school pictures, but she said no. She did not want me to have those pictures. When I went to walk away, Lou handed me the money I needed to pay for the pictures, but without her knowledge.

One day Sally needed a fix really bad and was sick. Lou went to rob a bank, and almost got busted, leaving her in the car to get caught. Jonathan, Peter, and Sally are now running from the law, having escaped to California.

Barringer High School was a tough school to attend. Anthony Imperial the activist was running for councilman and arrived at school with car loads of his supporters, making announcements with a bullhorn and causing the students to riot. The police force was called in and arrived with horses and with paddy wagons and beat the students with billy clubs. I was pregnant and running to get out of the way.

We were forced to accept harsh conditions, such as chains on the school doors, except for two in the front, which had police officers and guards to make sure that no one came or went without going through them. You were not permitted into the school without a picture ID card for that school. If you did not arrive on time, after the second bell you were considered absent; the guards would not allow you inside. I was pretty lucky as the black guard at the back door always permitted me inside the school after the second bell.

Our daughter Daniele was born on May 24, 1972, at the Columbus Hospital in Newark. It was now June a month later, when graduation was fast approaching.

The excitement of this great accomplishment had reached its peak. I was the first child out of thirteen children to graduate from high school. The joy of this occasion became overwhelming and I wanted to invite everyone in the family who was willing to attend, with the exception of Vicki and Grandma.

When I arrived at Mom's with the announcement, Dad disappeared into his den and stayed there the entire weekend, as he did on many occasions. Normally, when I arrived, I knocked on his door for a half hour or so, until he opened it. I sensed that he would not attend my graduation, so I did not bang on his door to make a fuss about it. Mother insisted that I make an attempt to invite him, otherwise, she said, she would not attend. I outright refused. This was one time he would not have the honor of saying no to me, as he did in the past. I knew Ma was not going to attend, even if I did ask him; she was not allowed to go anywhere without him, except to Attica Prison to visit James or some other prison to visit Jonathan, which was only once a year, when Susan or Vicki was able to take her.

When Sunday evening arrived, we were getting our belongings, bundling up the children, preparing to leave. Ma informed Dad of my disobedience, and as we were saying our goodbyes, he rushed out of the den to make an announcement: "If anyone attends this graduation, you better pack up your things and never return here again." Kelly and Joseph immediately stood up and said, "Let's go." They packed a few of their belongings and we all left. No one was afraid of him anymore, he was too old and unbelievable.

Kelly did my makeup and styled my hair for my graduation. Susan's husband drove me to the school because I had to arrive early. He also took about ten pictures of the graduation. Joseph, Kelly, Susan and her family, and Frank and my two babies attended my graduation.

Upon receiving my diploma, the principal and his assistant shook my hand and kissed me. I think they were just glad to be rid of me.

My graduation was soon forgotten, and Dad became more accustomed to my ways, proud that I now had an office job working in Newark at Bamberger's Department Store. He was older and more afraid, hiding in his locked den, tormented by his demons, and whenever weekend family visitors were around, pulling his own bad teeth out with a pliers. When he became ill, he refused to see a doctor—until the heart attacks began. When I arrived, I visited with everyone for a while, and then I knocked on his den door until he opened it. He did not open the door for anyone else, including Mom. If he wanted to see anyone, he came out of his room. Once I got into the tiny little room, he locked the door, keeping me in there for hours, serving me his fine liquor as we smoked; promising me that he had something special for me, only he couldn't remember where he put it. Amazingly enough,

I always hoped that he would actually give me something, but he never did.

When Dorothy was fourteen years of age, she decided to get away from Dad's control and moved in with me. She immediately got a boyfriend who was already married, and then had his child, causing me problems with his wife, who did not care to have any trouble with me. I made her stop seeing him, and then she found another boyfriend and persuaded me to move into his father's house, where there was a vacant apartment. It was getting hard to live in Parrot's house; she watched every move we made, so we did move down the street. Things got out of hand. There was no end to what you could in this four-story house. We began to indulge in wild living—gangs, drugs, alcohol, head music (hard rock), and Salsa music with continuous wild parties throughout the entire home. Different music playing on each floor, with students dancing and having a good time. Countless children from the high schools of Newark showed up rather than going to school.

Dorothy was not interested in going to Broadway Junior High, where I enrolled her. Dorothy's boyfriend's mother, who no longer lived there and was divorced, came by to threaten us with the police. The police arrived to raid the place with paddy wagons and police on horses. I was afraid of losing my children. The drug dealer Claudio said do not make a sound, and we all stayed quiet. The police stayed out there for about a half hour, and when they did not hear a sound, they left, assuming that it was a false alarm. I had a fling with Claudio, who gave me marijuana for free, and sometimes supplied the party with booze. That house, like the South Broadway apartment, was infested with rats and roaches. The rats were so numerous that they were not afraid of you and would run around underneath the table while you were eating dinner.

During one of our weekend visits at Mom's, the door bell rang. We all get excited whenever the doorbell rings, because it does not ring often. Opening the door, we discovered that Jonathan had arrived from California with a Jewish woman named Dora who had red hair and a face covered with freckles. Dad was in a good mood that day. Jonathan introduced her to Mom and Dad, and after about fifteen minutes, he left to go to the corner store, and didn't return , leaving Dora behind. She pestered him so much about meeting his parents that she bought the plane tickets, and they were on their way. He went back to California.

Dad was having a field day with her, while she sat on his lap being felt up by him. Ma did not like that at all. After a couple of days, Mom was fed up, saying, "I don't know where the hell this bitch came from, but I do know one thing, she is getting the hell out of my house." She saw me packing my things to leave, and said, "Nancy, you take her with you when you go." I answered, "Okay, Mom," and I did. She was a nymphomaniac, and although she stayed with me for two months, she hooked up with James, who had recently been released from Attica on leave. He spent that time with us, because of the freedom he had, as opposed to staying with our parents. He took this woman to New York City to prostitute for him; and when he went back to finish his sentence, she dated Joseph, who had been staying with us for a few months, until James was released from prison shortly afterwards.

We moved into a very nice security building up the hill. Dorothy hung out with prostitutes, and moved in with the Claudio, who turned out to be a very brutal man. He assaulted me one day, during my third pregnancy, while I was visiting her. When Vicki found out, she came into town with a carload of people, searching for him. When she could not find him, she went to his other woman's apartment and banged on the door, but he was not there. James arrived from New York in the middle of the night with a few of his buddies, gave the man a beating, and took his drugs and his leather jacket. Dorothy witnessed it. I too filed a police report, and had him arrested, forcing him to hire an attorney for his defense. After James left for California, this man assaulted

Dorothy, biting half her nipple off after learning that she saw her former boyfriend; she was forced to flee to California with Vicki and her family. Kelly came by to visit with her two children. After a couple of hours she stated that she needed to go to the corner store to purchase cigarettes. I did not see her again for another three weeks and I had to pay for a babysitter for my two children and her two children.

When she came back, I exploded. Why had she left her children with me? She got up and said, "See, I was nice about it to come and visit with you. Now, you are making it hard for me to stay here. I must leave. Good-bye."

Dad began to confide in me about things that troubled him, and things to come. One day during our visit in the den, he began to cry. I asked him, "Daddy why are you crying?" He answered, "I'm crying for you. The only reason why your Mother and everyone else is nice to you, is because of me. They all hate you because you're smart. They hate me, too." Mother asked me what we had talked about. I shook my head and said, "He's crazy." But I did not tell her what he said.

I felt sorry for Dad, because prior to Sally's departure, she cursed at him, saying things like, "Come on, old man. Chase me if you can." Attempting to run, he fell down on the ground with heart pains. No one was afraid of his threats anymore.

After Sally left for California, she and I wrote to each other, and she persuaded me to come to Los Angeles and that I could stay with her until I got settled. James and Dora made the same promise.

Frank and I decided to move to California to make a fresh start away from the overpopulated, drug- and crime-ridden city. We gave everything away except the clothing that we needed. In February of 1974, we boarded our flight to Los Angeles. Our son was three years of age, our daughter a year and a half, and I was nine months pregnant. Frank stayed behind for three months, to earn enough money to purchase a car. The evening prior to our departure, we visited Frank's parents to say our good-bye's. His father wept as he pretended to be sorry for his mistreatment towards me. We visited my parents to tell them that we were leaving. Dad was angry, bitter, scared, and very hurt to see me go. He tried his best to talk me out of it, but to no avail. In his den, he began to cry. I asked him why he was crying, and he hesitated once again, then he said, "I'm crying for what is going to happen to you when I die. They hate you, including your mother, and I fear for what they will do to you; but if you must go to California, please stay away from Vicki." I promised him that I would. Four years later, he passed away.

CHAPTER ELEVEN

Satan's Antics: Witchcraft and Phenomenal Experiences

Witchcraft was high on the list. Mother continued to tell stories about how James ran out of the room crying and screaming, proclaiming that he saw a lady with long blonde hair in the room and giving details of what she looked like. Mom said that when he was born, he had a caul over his head, indicating that he was a gifted child of God. I heard this story so many times told to outsiders who entered our home. Mom boasted about how wonderful it was to be able to see spirits, encouraging our belief in it. Mom explained that it was Grandma, Dad's mother, who was visiting him from the grave. Spirits were highly welcomed into the house, and perhaps invited. As years passed by, these occurrences became more frequent; and I realized many years later that this was Mother's excuse as to why Dad was up in the middle of the night assaulting James. She wanted him to feel comfortable about the incest that was going on between him and Dad, as if to say, "Son, I got your back." Just like she announced to everyone why Dad's homosexual friend traveled from Newark to Long Island, because he was hoping to see Vicki, whom he fell in love with when she was a teenager.

Ma constantly taught us the laws of superstitions. There were so many that they occupied a lot of our time. Everything that happened had something to do with superstition or witchcraft. After being drilled day and night, it was almost impossible to shake them off as unreal.

I had no idea that most of the occurrences were not just superstitions, but rather curses being sent back and forth from witches or sorcerers in the family. Mother frequently spoke about the curse Dad and Aunt Flora put on her leg and stomach. She had one large leg, filled with horrible fat varicose veins, and a very large stomach.

Demons were also a common word in conversations used at home. We were told that demons could have sex with us while we were sleeping, and this is believed to this day.

Children have a tendency to doodle. Our doodling at home consisted of pornographic drawings. I was taught how to draw naked bodies at a young age. Goosing (grabbing) each other in personal areas became so frequent that one could hardly believe it was indecent.

Dorothy had a problem concerning masturbation at a very young age. Not understanding, I informed Mother of this situation, and she told me to spank her whenever I caught her. Dorothy's problem became so out of control, that at any given moment, she would fall to the ground and begin to masturbate by putting her arm between her legs and rocking back and forth.

Ma did not need anyone investigating what was going on in our home. When I caught Dorothy outside engaged in this action, she ran for blocks for fear of receiving a a spanking. It was out of her control, as though something took over her body, throwing her down to the ground, exerting itself.

Whenever Mom and Dad thought that they were under any threat of a curse, they remained silent, as they drew themselves together. For instance, one day a dog began to howl, that meant someone was going to die. When nothing happened, they waited for the next sign to appear.

Ma saw a station wagon filled with nuns passing by as we were going down the highway. She got upset, claiming it was bad luck to see them, just as it was to receive a bouquet of flowers. "Throw them out the window! It's not time to die yet."

Dad, with his master plan to enforce evil in our lives, had no forewarning that Vicki was going to challenge him. Curses were sent back and forth between members of the family. Dad and Auntie, and sometimes Mom vs. Vicki.

One day Jonathan became deadly ill, and Dad and Mom rushed him to Auntie Flora to reverse the curse that Vicki placed on him. When I moved in with Susan, she informed me that Vicki had arrived at her home freaked out, proclaiming that roots were growing in her stomach and making Susan feel them. Sure enough, something that felt like roots were "growing" in her stomach. Auntie "reversed" the curse back to Vicki, and Jonathan became well again.

During my short stay with Vicki as a child, witchcraft was introduced to me. Vicki's father-in-law taught her how those powers worked. She made periodic visits to see him, taking me along most of the time.

On my first visit to her father-in-laws home, she took me to the kitchen where voo-doo and other practices were exercised. They showed me a few things, such as a glass of water and an apple that was placed on top of the refrigerator every day to feed the spirits. It was explained to me that they needed to be fed or they would go away. Supposedly, each morning the glass of water would be empty, and the apple would appear to be whole on the outside, but hollow inside.

Vicki excitedly showed me a glass that contained different oils. Inside the glass was a person's picture turned upside down. Ashes were underneath the glass indicating that something was burned under it. They tried to explain other things to me, but I was too young to understand. Her father-in-law began to threaten me each time we met about sending those evil spirits to get me if I ever spanked his grandson. I was induced with fear, when she began those practices in her home. On occasions when Vicki and her husband went out, leaving me to babysit, I sat by the table staring at the glass of water and the apple on top of the refrigerator, afraid to move because of the spirits. Years later, a family member told me that she had my picture turned upside down, with my eyes poked out, in some solution. I have no doubt.

During my stay with Auntie, I watched her read tea leaves for her clients. She served her clients a cup of tea in fine china. When the tea was half drunk, she tore the tea bag into the cup and after they drank the rest of the tea, she turned the cup upside down and a couple of minutes later she "read" the remaining leaves, predicting the future. The meeting lasted about twenty minutes. Auntie knew that I was watching, and after her clients left, I asked her questions about what she was doing, and why they left so much money on the table. She explained that she was paid well for her services because she revealed to them what numbers to play and what horses to bet on. Her information made them a lot of money, as Uncle and Dad also played numbers and betted on horses.

In later years, Vicki and Dorothy picked up the art of reading tea leaves. Dorothy came pretty close to being another "Auntie," so they say. Vicki also engaged in the crystal ball, along with other evils.

I had to listen to Susan's endless ghost stories, which haunted her. She was overwhelmed by their presence and they were constantly on her mind. She knew exactly what they would do, and the hour when they would do it; for instance, at eight o'clock in the evening, the rocking chair started to rock, and at other times there was knocking on the walls and banging on the pipes. Her desperate desire to prove that she was not crazy caused her to keep me up late at night, waiting to hear them with her. She said that she really freaked out when her toddler children started playing with them when her husband was at work. I did not know what to think. I had experienced almost everything in the past fourteen years, living on this planet; but certainly not ghosts, other than the stories Jonathan and James told many years earlier in the haunted house. I am about to enter a new realm.

Susan's husband reassured me that she was imagining everything. He said the building was old, and that is why the walls and the pipes made banging sounds.

One night while everyone was asleep in that small apartment where Susan, her family and I lived, I was undressing, getting ready for bed, when I heard a loud whistle of approval. I quickly turned around and peeped into the room a few feet away to see if my brother-in-law was up, and there he was, sound asleep, snoring next to my sister. I know for a fact that it was a spirit.

When we moved from that small apartment in Newark to the two-bedroom house in Laurence Harbor, New Jersey, one night while Susan and her husband were asleep, I quietly entered their dark bedroom to get a hair brush from her vanity. Suddently the organ lit up and began to play music. I freaked out, and jumped into their bed. They woke up and witnessed what I saw and heard. Susan was so happy that I was joining her in her nightmare and excited that for the first time her husband also got to experience something phenomenal.

When Susan arrived for her weekend visit, she anxiously blurted out her ghost adventures from the previous week. Dad took pleasure in hearing every detail, laughing behind her back. Undoubtedly he and Auntie were involved in that deal. Dad could not have her for himself, and would not let her find peace with anyone else. To this day, she remains haunted by those spirits and talks to them constantly.

From that time on, everyone was proclaiming phenomenal experiences. James's pregnant wife stated that while walking down the stairs to the first floor of the house, a broomstick came out of nowhere, causing her to trip and almost fall. Others said blankets were pulled off the bed while they were sleeping, and told of being punched through the mattress.

Everyone knew that our family was under a curse. I was able to escape the "curse" through being born again—into another family. The family of God. Thank you, Lord.

We women suffered during our menstrual cycles, which sometimes lasted for months, with large blood clots; and other times it did not arrive again for many months. Susan suffered the most, and was in and out of the hospital for "scrapings" as she called it.

Never knowing when or if we were pregnant, abortion became a popular thing with Ma. She encouraged her daughters to use remedies that might work, such as eating excess amounts of Ex-lax, and drinking an overabundance of cod liver oil while soaking in a hot tub.

Vicki told us about her abortion experience in New York City, in an abandoned building, giving us the ugly, gruesome details such as a coat hanger which was used to rip the fetus out of her body. She assumed death awaited her, due to this illegal, unprofessional process.

I was never introduced to a birth control pill; just condoms, which were unreliable. One time I missed my menstrual cycle and assumed that I was pregnant, never seeing a doctor to verify it.

Kelly often came to New Jersey to visit her boyfriend from Pakistan who was here studying to become a doctor. She also visited me, especially when she needed a babysitter, leaving her children with me for a couple of weeks when it was supposed to be for a few hours.

During one of these visits, I told her that I might be pregnant. She took me to a woman doctor in town who performed illegal abortions out of a small apartment. Upon entering the small kitchen, the door was shut, and I undressed. The round white tin bowl with the stagnant pinkish colored water that contained the operation tools remain vaguely in my mind. She injected a needle into my vagina, placed a tool up into it, and within five minutes we were on our way.

A few days later, I arrived at her office with a friend and discovered that she had moved. After knocking on the door for a short while, a black man answered; apparently, we woke him up, as he stood there scratching his head and rubbing his eyes. A few other people were also in the room. I said, "Excuse me, I was looking for a doctor's office." He responded, "No ma'am, they ain't no doctor's office here. No sir. I 've been here 'bout a few months, and ain't no doctor been here." I apologized for the inconvenience and left.

CHAPTER TWELVE

The Funeral March

In the early afternoon of the twelfth of December, 1977, Kelly telephoned my home in Hawthorne, California. He voice sounded troubled as she said, "Daddy is dead." I answered her, "Kelly, please do not lie like that. That's nothing to play around with." "It's true, I swear to God it's true," she insisted. If someone in the family swore to God, it was almost sure that they were telling the truth. She said that Mother could not come to the corner pay phone because she was a nervous wreck; and she began to cry. I asked her if Susan and Vicki knew, and she answered, "Yes. I just got off the phone with them." She said that she would call me back later so that I could make arrangements to fly to New York. I telephoned Susan and Vicki to verify Kelly's story.

Within the hour, most of the family had flocked to my house, worried about how they would get enough money to fly to New York. Everyone knew not to go to Susan or Vicki for help. Those two would not dream of helping anyone financially; besides, they knew that no one would pay them back.

There was a lot of excitement that day and Kelly called collect many times. Each person wanted to hear the whole story. Kids were running around the house, babies crying, music blasting, and the phone ringing. Glasses of wine were continually passed around. The place was a madhouse. I was a nervous wreck, with everyone depending on me to get them to New York, when I had no money myself. At the moment, I could not think about how I was going to get there, as I was too involved consulting each person, and hanging in there until each one made his or her plans.

Finally, James was the only one left, other than myself, who had not acquired funds. Everyone else had booked their flights, and the plane was scheduled to leave in the evening. James was crying and begging me to please not leave without him and to help him get to New York. Hugging him, I told him that I would not leave without him. Just then, another collect phone call came in from Kelly, stating that Mom had purchased a ticket for James. He leaped for joy as Kelly sent Mother's regret for not being able to help me. James kissed me and said he loved me. He soon was out the door, and on his way to the airport with the rest of the nine family members who lived in California.

Now the house was quiet and Frank arrived home from work. I explained everything to him and then I telephoned Susan, discovering that she and Vicki had already left for the airport. Susan's husband knew that everyone had already left and that I needed money to pay for my fare. He turned everyone else down who asked him for cash. He said, "I know that you are good for it, and I am not concerned about getting it back. I'll be right over with the money you need to get you there, under one condition. Do not tell anyone that I lent you this money. Certainly, do not tell Susan, she will have a fit. Knowing how deep rooted her hatred developed towards me, I'll tell her when she returns from New York." I agreed, and within thirty minutes, he arrived with the cash.

I telephoned my friend Joan and told her I had to leave town. She agreed to take care of the children during the day, while Frank was at work. She took the children to school, and cared for the youngest one during the day.

Next, I drove to the Lee Strauss Institute, where I was presently studying acting, and asked the director to telephone

Mrs. Strauss, who was presently living in New York, and ask her to lend me enough money to get back from New York after I attended my father's funeral. She agreed, and the director said to me, "You have a lot of balls kiddo, asking to borrow money." Nevertheless, he handed it over. He was very fond of me, and so was Mrs. Strauss.

I made it to the airport just before the plane left. Eleven family members, including Latasha's husband, went to New York for the funeral. Dorothy and Tonya departed from Fresno, where they lived together. Latasha and her husband, who were hype cocaine junkies, took a later flight from Los Angeles.

We boarded the plane and took our seats, realizing that our family was the only group seated in that section. It almost seemed like we were the only ones in the airplane. Feeling a little high from drinking wine, and remembering that Susan had never flown before and was afraid, I asked her if she was okay. She answered, "I'm okay," in a scared tone. A few minutes later I repeated the question and told her that all was well. Joseph rudely interrupted, telling me to shut up. I replied that I didn't have to shut up. I began to talk to Susan again when Joseph rudely interrupted, threatening to punch me in the mouth. I could not believe this sudden hatred. Everyone had behaved in a mannerly way at my home, and now all of a sudden, I was being spoken to aggressively. James told Joseph to cool out as the stewardess arrived with her cart. I ordered a shot of whiskey for James and myself; and when we finished, I ordered another round for us. When I turned around to ask Susan how she was doing, Joseph acted as tough, as if he wanted to get physical with me, but James told him to quit.

Venturing from my seat, I swayed to the room where the flight attendants hung out. They knew we were going to Dad's funeral and I sat conversing with them, as though I was a part of their group. After a while they got a member of the family to escort me back to my seat. Staggering back down the corridor, I made it back to my seat and soon passed out.

Four hours later, James was shaking me, trying to wake me up. "Leave me alone and let me sleep," I said. He replied, "We're in New York, Nancy, and we have to leave the plane." When I heard New York, my eyes opened, and to my surprise, James and I were the only passengers left on the plane. Excitedly, I got up and we exited.

Mother and Kelly were at Kennedy Airport to greet us. While waiting for our luggage, Susan and Vicki began spilling their guts about how I misbehaved on the airplane. We all crammed into one car, and Joseph threatened me until we arrived at Mom's home. He made an oath that we were going to do battle before this trip ended.

Grandma was left at the house to guard the treasures Dad had supposedly hidden in his den locker all these years. She kept a commanding attitude, apparently ready and willing to physically hurt anyone seeking to get their hands on the loot, Dad's stolen property that he collected for years. After guarding the den for two days and nights, she discovered that her effort was in vain. Jonathan and our cousins had already cut the bars on the den window, busted open the locker, and raided the goods. Mother was heartbroken, but could only curse at the boys, who could have cared less.

Sally and I were kind of close at this time, due to my raising her daughter for three and a half years without any financial contribution from her. After giving Mother some money, ninety dollars was left over to get me through my ten-day stay. Not wanting to keep the rest of the money in my possession, I entrusted Sally to give it to Mom to hold for me.

Later in the day, I asked Ma to let me have ten dollars of my money. She answered, "What money?" I said, "The money I had you hold for me." She said, "What money did you have me hold for you?" I responded, "Didn't Sally give you the ninety dollars to hold for me?" She said, "Sally gave me nothing to hold for you. She just left for New York with Frank, Gene, and your brothers."

I knew then that I would never see my money. Frank, our cousin, was a big time junkie, and so were Sally and the boys. They went to Harlem to score "black tar" (heroin). I was left penniless for the next nine days, and it was going to be hell for me.

I had been studying acting for about three years, taking modern dance classes, and my dance Instructor embarrassed me for about nine months in front of the class, until I straightened my shoulders and stood upright. I was being shaped into someone special, different from what I was raised to be. Praise God!

In my luggage was the most beautiful black apparel, enough to dress differently each day during my stay. I decided that not a soul was going to find out that I was broke; especially with "high society" Aunt Flora and her sons hanging around. Dad's other sister and family, who considered themselves at an even higher standard than Aunt Flora's, also made their presence known.

I had acquired a friend named Victoria Marie, whom I met at the Strauss Institute, a blonde, hazel-eyed "Jewish princess," who was my best friend for many years. Since we were the same size (eight), she furnished me with all her clothing, shoes that she had made, makeup, and whatever else she thought I needed to have to be up to par with her. My appearance was astonishing, with my finely styled hair, which complimented me even further. One would think that I had deserted a movie set to indulge in this fiasco. I lent some of my clothes to my sisters, so that they too could have the proper attire for this occasion. We needed to keep up with the Joneses, so to speak.

The morning after our arrival, Mother, Kelly, Jonathan, and I went to the hospital to claim the body. We stood in front of a window at the end of the South Bay Shore Hospital corridor that was covered with a drape. We four stood there gazing at the drape, when suddenly the drape was drawn back, displaying Dad on a table with his mouth wide open in shock, as though he saw a legion of demons arriving to take him down to hell. Kelly let out an unbearable scream, falling down to the floor, and Jonathan and

Mom grabbed her arms to hold her up. Quickly, the drapes were drawn shut. While Kelly's performance continued, and I turned the knob of the first door nearest the window, and it opened. I entered the cold room where Dad's body lay, and stared at him, making sure he was really dead. Feeling morbid, I left the room. When I told Ma what I had done, she was amazed, repeating it to Jonathan and Kelly.

Susan's husband rented her a car, and Grandma, Ma, Susan, and Vicki became a team, doing everything together. Sometimes Grandma stayed home to watch the fortress. My stay at Mom's became unsafe for me, with Joseph threatening my life and I without any money. I telephoned my husband's brother, who lived in Newark, to tell him I was coming over. I asked Aunt Flora if I could get a ride to the city with her, and she agreed to take me. I took my suitcase and was ready to leave with her when her two sons, Gene and Frank (known for being in the Mafia), asked their mother where I was going. She told them that she had agreed to take me into the city. Gene, who was very tall and handsome, immediately said, "She isn't going anywhere! She has a funeral to attend." Frank said, "Yeah, that's right. She isn't going anywhere." Everyone knew that Auntie was a strong person, and a woman of her word, so Uncle and all the men in the family except Joseph left, leaving Auntie and I stranded at the house. The next day, Uncle returned for her. That day he saw the endless harassment that Joseph was giving me.

Joseph got in my face, and just when he was about to physically abuse me, Grandma told him to stop and Uncle stood up in my defense, grabbing Joseph by the throat and holding him up against the wall. Joseph and Uncle are very tall men, but Joseph was shook up. Uncle then took Auntie home.

There were times when the house was full of people, and at other times quiet, with only a few members of the family around. It was hard to go anywhere in below-zero weather, without resources. My outing consisted of running to the corner to make a collect call to my husband Frank to inform him of the latest news, and then running back to the house before the tears froze on my face.

Mother and her gang always went out to eat, and there was no food in the house. I went a couple of days without eating or sleeping with the exception of a few hours while Dorothy guarded me, when Joseph was not around; for fear that he would injure me while I was asleep. He was still annoyed at my behavior on the airplane during our flight to New York, and threatened to assault me. His words to me was "You have to sleep sometime."

A neighbor brought some cold cuts and bread to the house. The house was quiet, and I said to myself, "I'm almost starved to death, I'm so glad I finally get to eat something." I made myself a sandwich, and just as I sat down to take a bite, Grandma entered the dinning room and said, "Watcha got in there? How much meat and cheese you put in that sandwich? Don't you be taking too much now, you didn't bring that food in here, and other peoples got to eat too!" She was not aware of the tears that rushed to my eyes, and I felt like I wanted to vomit. Between the hunger, endless threats on my life, my stolen funds, Mother's total lack of interest in my welfare, and my physical exhaustion from lack of sleep, I felt like I was going to collapse. All I could think of is, "Be strong, it will soon be all over and I can go back to my beautiful home and be with my husband and my children."

Dad was deceased for five days and the time was growing nearer for his burial. Relatives were arriving from everywhere, including a half brother and half sisters that I did not know existed. To my surprise, they were almost the same ages as my siblings. They even sang the same foreign songs Dad taught us. I asked Mother what was going on, and who these people were and how did this fit together? Mom said, "It's all over now. He's dead." "What are you trying to say?" I asked. She sat down and told me the story as Susan, Vicki, and some other intermediate members listened. "Well, you see, your father was married four times. When he married me, the government caught up with him, and charged him with bigamy, because he was married to this other woman and me at the same time." She smiled as she reminisced. "They told him he'd better make up his mind who he wanted to be married to." Then she said something in reference to his green card. "I was seven months pregnant with you when your Dad and I were married legally. You were the first legitimate child born."

I smiled and looked at Susan and Vicki, who were both fit to be tied. From that point on, I received even worst treatment from Susan and Vicki. The only time we were nice to each other was when the outside family was around.

Our half brother and sisters were scrutinizing us. They sang the foreign songs Dad taught them and they spoke about how he sent them to ballet school. This also explains where everything Dad confiscated from me went, baby clothes, furniture, and everything else.

It was quite obvious what had gone on. Mom was sharing Dad with his other wife and children. For many years she lied to us, saying that he had to leave the family for months due to his profession as a contractor. As the story went, he built high rises, and most of his work was in Canada; which explains the long leaves of absence. Since she took all of this so comfortably, with his other children arriving at their home, I figured that she also knew and visited these other children. Now that I recollect, I remember seeing their faces in high school graduation pictures Dad displayed in his small den. In spite of Mother's hatred towards me, she never failed to keep my high school graduation picture on the table next to her side of the bed, and Jonathan's navy picture was placed on Dad's table, in spite of the fact that Jonathan went AWOL and spent the duration of his enlistment in prison. Susan and Vicki despised that fact, as their pictures, and their family's, were forbidden inside the house.

The house was crowded with relatives and a few friends. Auntie Blanche's two daughters also arrived bearing food out of their respect for their mother. They were too "above" us to hold much conversation. Especially with me, knowing that their mother had high regards concerning me. Aunt Flora's only daughter, the "project princess," did not show up. A lot of action was going on, as they brought in all kinds of food and drinks. Gene brought in five black men of British descent. They were dressed in suits, played instruments, and sang beautifully. Their accent was so strong, it seemed as though they just got off the boat. He must have hired them to serenade the funeral crowd or us female cousins. I sat near the piano, and every one of us girls looked great.

Mother knew that everyone looked on her as a degenerate, and made her way through the crowd, announcing, "Did you know that Nancy is an actress? She's studying with that famous instructor, what's his name? Lee Strauss. That guy taught"—and she proceeded to mention the name of five stars who had studied under him. Although she mispronounced the director's name, everyone knew who she was referring to. Gene said in an unimpressed tone, "I know of the guy." Being jealous of that statement, the cousins politely ignored me, treating me as though I was not in the room. I continued sitting prim and proper, knowing that I had everyone's attention and that I had a reputation to maintain.

Gene lifted up an expensive bottle of liquor, announcing to everyone that Dorothy and he page were the only ones who were going to drink it later on. After he left, I whispered in uncle Dillion's ear, "Where did Gene hide his bottle of liquor?" He told me where it was—behind a chair. I thanked and kissed him on the cheek. When no one was looking, I quickly opened the bottle and poured myself a drink. After about ten trips to the hiding place, the bottle was empty. Gene returned to celebrate with Dorothy, only to discover that the bottle was bone dry. He became outraged, his Mafia attitude exploded as he attempted to find out who the culprit was. I began to panic, and because I did not move around much or speak much to anyone when outside family was around, it was hard to detect my behavior. Everyone was subjected to this outburst. Being the only person who was high, It should have been obvious that it was me. My biggest concern was that Uncle would reveal to him that it was me. Our eyes met a few times as I tried to signal him not to tell. I whispered in his ear, "Uncle, please do not tell him that it was me." He said, "Of course not." He and everyone else knew that they were never going see us again; we were not close relatives, being the outcasts of the clan, and now living thousands of miles away.

The following day day Gene took a cheap shot at me. He joined Susan and I in the dining room as he proceeded to share with Susan that he would be in Los Angeles soon and that she was one of the first people he intended to visit. He repeated this statement three more times in my presence, with other family members. He never held a conversation with me in my lifetime. Obviously, he was intimidated by my presence.

One day I was alone in the kitchen cooking, when Frank entered and shut the door. He said to me, "I know what the hell you are doing in Hollywood with Lee Strauss. You are sucking his dick, is what you are doing. How else can you get near a man like that?" He went and sat down at the dining room table. I began to laugh and sing, turning my back to him, waving my hands back and forth: "Shine on, shine on harvest moon, way in the sky." Then I bent over and stuck my rear end out at him. He is very tall and I am size seven. He jumped up and chased me and I ran toward Mom's bedroom screaming, "Ma! Ma!" I got into her room just in time. He knew not to cross that threshold.

Joseph freaked out and stayed in the den for hours, trying to "communicate" with Dad. As Joseph knocked on the wall the beat was returned to establish that he had communicated with Dad. Everyone wanted to be in the den because they had a message for him. Mother was enthused that Dad was still around, as she always believed that you stay on the earth for three days before going to your final destination.

Sally entered the crowded living room totally naked and dripping wet, requesting a towel. Mom yelled at her to get back into the bathroom. Latasha claimed she had to leave the house after taking a "bloody" shower. She said that when she turned the shower on, blood came out. They must have taken some bad drugs.

Fights began to break out between the guys, resulting in broken car windows and other incidents. Frank slapped one of Kelly's boys, almost causing a rumble. Gene took his gun out to show authority and Uncle Angel, Ma's brother, arrived from Glendale, California in the mist of all this.

Auntie Flora and Auntie Blanche, Dad's sister's, were feuding since before I was born. They could never be under the same roof at the same time. When Auntie Blanche was at the house visiting, Aunt Flora had to wait a few blocks away until she left, and vice versa. Usually, one of their children would appear to let the other aunt know that their mother was waiting outside. Whenever Auntie Blanche arrived, everyone crowded around to greet her, as she was the most highly respected person in the family into her eighties. She called out for me, "Where is Nancy? I want to see Nancy." I answered, "Here I am, Auntie Blanche." She reached out her hand for mine. "Let us sit in a place where we can talk." "Okay, Auntie."

No one would dare spy on us, or give any indication of disapproval. We sat next to each other in the living room, holding hands as she said, "You're the only one. Your father says that you're the only one. The rest of them are worthless. Be careful of them, my child, do you hear?" I said yes. Since her last stroke, her whole body shook continuously. Her jaw was twisted to the side, forcing her to speak with a twang. Everyone was on their best behavior when she was around. She said a few more words, when suddenly their was a knock on the door. As the door opened a woman appeared holding a cake in her hands. Mrs. Javitz was the woman who lived across the street, whom I've never seen before.

Auntie said, "That's the woman who killed my brother! She has the nerve to show her face around here after she killed my brother!" She began to weep, "Oh God, oh God." I tried to comfort her. That neighbor had nothing to do with Dad's death. It was by coincidence that he happened to have a heart attack after giving her a lift to the hospital.

Mother told the story of what happened to Dad. "He knew it was his time to go, and he never wanted to go anywhere without me. He was so afraid, and if I was in the yard, or maybe in the bathroom too long, he would call my name, asking me where I was and what was taking me so long. For the last four months we did everything together, when I was not at work. He began to look and feel very good. A month ago, he gazed into the mirror and made a joke about how great he felt; and that he was going to fool everyone by living many more years. Then Mrs. Levin, the neighbor across the street, came to the door crying that she felt sick, and needed a ride to the the Bay Shore Hospital. I told your father, 'I'll hurry up and get dressed,' but he said no, that he'd be all right. He drove Mrs. Javitz to the hospital and dropped her off in the parking lot. She said goodbye, and quickly went into the hospital. This is when it happened. They found your father lying on the ground near the car. Apparently, as Mrs. Javitz rushed into the hospital, your father had a heart attack. He opened the car door and when he tried to walk, he fell dead on the ground. I remember standing on the porch waving goodbye as he drove down the street. I watched until I couldn't see him anymore.

"That was the first time I ever stood watching him drive away until I couldn't see him anymore. It was as though, somehow, I knew I would never see him again." Then Mother became outraged, as she explained how they left him lying on the ground for six hours before contacting her. She said that the policemen stole eighty dollars from his pocket, and other personal items.

Neighbors arrived to show their respect, and the black boy name Larry, now a man, whose name I wrote a thousand times, arrived with his mother, Mrs. Green and little sister knick named Kissy, as he was their driver. He stood quietly in the living room next to the front door. I usually sat on the piano bench next to the piano that was not far from the front door, to observe everyone who entered the house. I immediately stood up to approach Mrs. Green and her fifteen-year-old daughter "Kissy." It had been about twelve years since I had seen them last. I glanced at Larry and he acknowledged me as we said, "Hi." I began to reminisce about how I was sent away, and wondered what life would have been like if things had turned out differently. He was still a quiet gentleman. I sensed that he recognized my beauty and was amazed at what a fine lady I had turned out to be.

The young woman who tried to steal my husband from me shortly after our marriage, also arrived. I was suspicious of her visit, thinking she had come hoping to see my husband.

Family members and some friends gathered at the morgue for the wake. Reverend Johnson spoke a few words about Dad and weeping filled the room. Auntie Blanche stayed with me in the front row, holding my hand and saying, "Your father said that you are the only one. The only one." Ma sat in the back row, as though she had no place to be amongst the elite, or as if to say that she was not his wife. Larry, his mother, and sister also attended. I refused to shed one tear for this occasion, and it seemed that Larry and I were the only ones who were not sad as we glanced at each other for a moment.

Now it was time for each person to say their last farewells to Dad. Vicki stayed near the casket at all times, and when each of us reached the casket, she took her hands and shoved us away, acting as though she was in charge. The casket was then closed and Mother entered an old worn-out limousine with her gang. The rest of us piled into available cars. We all followed the limousine, passing Ma's house first, and then on our way to the Bay Shore cemetery. It was close to zero on this eighteenth day of December. We stood at the grave site and Reverend Johnson spoke once again. Auntie Blanche's daughters and other family members felt sorry for us California ladies, because no attire could stop us from shivering with our teeth chattering in that kind of weather. Our cousin Marie said, "Poor things, their blood is so thin." That was the kindest thing she spoke towards us in years. She was said to be a doctor.

We each were handed a red carnation to place on top of the casket. Kelly let out her last scream, as though she wanted to be buried with him. We all got into the cars, and as we were leaving, we looked back to see another funeral party waiting to approach. Looking closely, we recognized that Aunt Flora was waiting for Auntie Blanche to leave the scene so that she could take her turn mourning her brother.

Only the immediate family returned to Mom's house. We got our things together and the next day we were ready to go back to Los Angeles. Joseph refused to let us leave in peace. He caused a lot of problems, assaulting Vicki, grabbing her by the throat, and lifting her up in the air. Feeling sorry for her, I took my suitcase and stood outside with her until we all left a half hour later.

Vicki and I could not get enough good-byes with Mom at the airport, and missed our flight. Susan and the others left without us. We caught the next flight fifteen minutes later.

I never returned to his grave. He was buried in a numbered grave without a tombstone. He died like a bum in the street, and it was not long before I was to find out what his tears meant for me, about Mother's hatred (and the rest of the family's) toward me. The things he was trying to prepare for me were about to take place in the near future. My new nightmare of rejection and abuse from family members, awaits me.

www.ingramcontent.com/pod-product-compliance
Lightning Source LLC
Chambersburg PA
CBHW051835040426
42447CB00006B/537

9780615503523